D1757394

WAITING ROOM GERMANY
Klaus Pohl

STRANGER'S HOUSE
Dea Loher

THE TABLE LAID
Anna Langhoff

JENNIFER KLEMM
D. Rust

Other Volumes in the International Collection

AUSTRALIA PLAYS
ed. Katharine Parsons
Jack Davis: *No Sugar*
Alma de Groen:
The Rivers of China
Michael Gow: *Away*
Louis Nowra: *The Golden Age*
David Williamson:
Travelling North
ISBN 1 85459 056 1

THE CRACK IN THE EMERALD
New Irish Plays ed. David Grant
Dermot Bolger:
The Lament for Arthur Cleary
Marina Carr: *Low in the Dark*
Michael Harding: *The Misogynist*
Marie Jones: *The Hamster Wheel*
ISBN 1 85459 237 8

CZECH PLAYS
ed. Barbara Day
Vaclav Havel: *Tomorrow!*
Ivan Klima: *Games*
Josef Topol: *Cat on the Rails*
Daniela Fischerova: *Dog and Wolf*
ISBN 1 85459 074 X

DUTCH PLAYS
ed. Della Couling
Lodewijk de Boer:
The Buddha of Ceylon
Judith Herzberg:
The Wedding Party
Arne Sierens: *Drummers*
Karst Woudstra: *Burying the Dog*
Frans Strijards:
The Stendhal Syndrome
ISBN 1 85459 289 0

HUNGARIAN PLAYS
ed. László Upor
András Nagy. *The Seducer's Diary*
Andor Szilágyi: *Unsent Letters*
Ákos Németh: *Muller's Dances*
Péter Kárpáti: *Everywoman*
ISBN 1 85459 244 0

LATIN AMERICAN PLAYS
ed. Sebastian Doggart
Octavio Paz: *Rapaccini's Daughter*
Jose Triana: *Night of the Assassins*
Griselda Gambaro: *Saying Yes*
Carlos Fuentes:
Orchids in the Moonlight
Mario Vargas Llosa:
Mistress of Desires
ISNB 1 85459 249 1

SCOT-FREE
New Scottish Plays
ed. Alasdair Cameron
John Byrne: *Writer's Cramp*
John Clifford: *Losing Venice*
Anne Marie Di Mambro:
The Letter-Box
Chris Hannan:
Elizabeth Gordon Quinn
John McKay: *Dead Dad Dog*
Rona Munro:
Saturday at the Commodore
Tony Roper: *The Steamie*
ISBN 1 85459 017

SOUTH AFRICAN PLAYS
ed. Stephen Gray
Anthony Akerman:
Somewhere on the Border
Maishe Maponya:
The Hungry Earth
Susan Pam-Grant:
Curl Up and Dye
Paul Slabolepszy: *Over the Hill*
Pieter-Dirk Uys: *Just Like Home*
ISBN 1 85459 148 7

STARS IN THE MORNING SKY
ed. Michael Glenny
Alexander Chervinsky:
Heart of a Dog
Alexander Galin:
Stars in the Morning Sky
Alexander Gelman:
A Man with Connections
Grigory Gorin: *Forget Herostratus!*
Ludmila Petrushevskaya:
Three Girls in Blue
ISBN 1 85459 020 0

GERMAN PLAYS

Plays from a Changing Country

Selected and edited by Elyse Dodgson

KLAUS POHL ■ WAITING ROOM GERMANY

Translated by David Tushingham

DEA LOHER ■ STRANGER'S HOUSE

Translated by David Tushingham

ANNA LANGHOFF ■ THE TABLE LAID

Translated by David Spencer

D. RUST ■ JENNIFER KLEMM

Translated by Rosee Riggs

Introduction by David Tushingham

THE INTERNATIONAL COLLECTION

NICK HERN BOOKS
London

in association with the Goethe-Institut

and the Royal Court Theatre

A Nick Hern Book

German Plays first published in Great Britain in 1997
as an original paperback by Nick Hern Books Limited,
14 Larden Road, London W3 7ST

Typeset by Country Setting, Woodchurch, Kent TN26 3TB

Printed and bound in Great Britain
by Athenaeum Press Ltd, Gateshead, Tyne & Wear

A CIP catalogue record for this book is available from
the British Library

ISBN 1 85459 338 2

Contents

For Gerd

*who first introduced me to
the idea of German exchange.*

e.d.

Preface

The plays collected in this volume were first presented to a British audience at a German Playreading Season at the Royal Court Theatre in 1995. The season of *New German Voices* was part of an ongoing British-German theatre project which involves the Royal Court Theatre and the Goethe-Institut London on one side of the channel and the Deutsches Theater Berlin as well as the British Council on the other.

What makes this exchange so gratifying and successful is its truly bi-lateral character. While contemporary German plays and their authors are presented to British audiences, British playwrights and their works are also introduced to German audiences in Berlin through the Deutsches Theater. And, of course, the readings are accompanied by an exchange of ideas and attitudes regarding theatre traditions, audience expectations and support for new writing in both countries.

Contemporary theatre is probably the art form that registers most directly social, political, cultural challenges of our time. In a very concrete way, the actual theatrical experience confronts us with the way we live, the ways in which we relate to each other. The plays in this selection of *New German Voices: Plays from a Changing Country* reflect the new climate that has arisen in Germany since unification in very different ways and using a diversity of approaches. In this way they may provide a more complex and multifacetted mirror of current issues than comes across in the mass media.

The plays presented here are by writers who are in the process of establishing themselves in Germany. With its long tradition of encouraging and supporting new writing for the stage, the Royal Court is, of course, an ideal partner. Many of today's most distinguished British playwrights had early works produced there. Through this project, the Royal Court now gives young German writers a chance to see their plays in an international context to find out whether they 'translate' into a context outside their own linguistic and cultural sphere.

Of the five plays presented at the German Season in 1995 three will have had a fully fledged production in London at the time of publication. Making the plays available in print may, we hope, pave the way for further stage productions.

Helga Wilderotter-Ikonomou

Head of Programme Department
Goethe-Institut London

Foreword

The Royal Court Theatre has been the home of new theatre writing in Britain since the English Stage Company under George Devine took up residence there in 1956. In their very first season – which famously included the premiere of *Look Back in Anger* – there was a play from outside Britain, and it is significant that it came from Germany: the first production in English of Bertolt Brecht's *The Good Woman of Setzuan*, directed by George Devine with a cast that included Peggy Ashcroft, John Osborne and Joan Plowright. In the nineties new international writing continues to flourish at the Royal Court, and once again the idea of exchanging new plays with theatres in other countries began with writers from Germany.

The idea of an exchange with new German writers began in 1992 when I met with a group of young playwrights studying at the Hochschule der Künste, Berlin, who became excited by the process of developing new plays at the Royal Court. One of them was Dea Loher, who developed her first play *Olga's Room (Olga's Raum)* as part of the 1993 Royal Court International Summer School and whose *Stranger's House (Fremdes Haus)* appears in this volume. Many of the young writers I met at this time were attracted to the Royal Court because they felt it offered them a unique opportunity to collaborate with a director on the early drafts of their play. For the last four years playwrights, directors and dramaturgs have come to the Royal Court to work with us. These exchanges coincided with a time that is now seen as a renaissance in new writing in the British theatre with first plays by a new generation which included Jez Butterworth, Nick Grosso, Sarah Kane, Ayub Khan-Din, Martin McDonagh, Conor McPherson, Joe Penhall, Rebecca Prichard, Mark Ravenhill, Judy Upton and Michael Wynne. We decided to look for their German counterparts as we realised that other leading British theatres had already introduced British audiences to the important and influential work of major German contemporary playwrights such as Franz Xaver Kroetz, Peter Handke, Heiner Müller, and Botho Strauss. We wanted to concentrate on the young writers who were unknown here but were beginning to emerge in Germany.

In October 1993, our first series of readings of new German plays took place in the Royal Court Theatre Upstairs. After the week of readings we decided to find a partner who would ensure the continuity of the project and allow us to take part in a genuine exchange of ideas. We approached many theatres in Germany and received the most enthusiastic response at the Deutsches Theater Berlin from Michael Eberth, who was then the chief dramaturg. We decided that we would be partners in future exchanges.

In October 1994 five Royal Court playwrights – Martin Crimp, Kevin Elyot. David Greig, Meredith Oakes and David Spencer – had their work translated into German and given rehearsed readings in Berlin. All five writers, our literary manager, artistic director Stephen Daldry and I took part in the *Woche der Englischen Dramatik*, with the support of the British Council. Fiery discussions about our strengths and our differences began as the British contingent joined a panel to discuss new writing in both countries. Our most lively arguments centred on different attitudes to the writer-director relationship and the role of the writer and dramaturg in the rehearsal process. The small 'Baracke' theatre was packed with an audience throughout the week, and ideas were explored long into the night. As a result, productions of several of these plays took place in different parts of Germany, and both theatres began to prepare for a second round of exchanges.

In October 1995 the Royal Court presented a second series of rehearsed readings of new plays from Germany, again with the Goethe Institut in London, entitled *Plays from a Changing Country*. This time we decided with our partner theatre to look at new plays written in the previous five years that explored the change in Germany since the Berlin Wall came down in 1989. The writers Klaus Chatten, Anna Langhoff, Dea Loher, Klaus Pohl and D. Rust all took part in rehearsals of their plays in London and spent a week with us in the Theatre Upstairs.

Following this second series of readings three plays had a
further life in London, including a production at the Royal
Court Theatre Downstairs of Klaus Pohl's *Waiting Room
Germany* (*Wartesaal Deutschland*), produced in November
1995 to critical acclaim within weeks of its world premiere at
the Deutsches Theater Berlin. Klaus Chatten's *Sugar Dollies*
(*Prunksitzung*), which for copyright reasons cannot be
included in this volume, was the success of the 1996 season
at the Deutsches Theater and was produced at the Gate Theatre
in London in the same year. Anna Langhoff's *The Table Laid*
(*Transit Heimat: Gedeckte Tische*) had a two week workshop
at the Royal Court and a presentation of the work-in-progress
at the Arts Depot in April 1997.

As the British and German writers develop this ongoing dia-
logue there are increasing possibilities for further collaborations.
In February 1997 the Baracke of the Deutsches Theater began
a highly successful programme of new international work, and
once again the British writers were invited to Berlin to hear
readings of their work translated into German. With the help of
the British Council, Jim Cartwright, Phyllis Nagy, Sarah Kane
and Mark Ravenhill were invited to Berlin for the second
Royal Court week at the Baracke. As a result of this highly
successful event, future productions of these plays are planned
at the Deutsches Theater and other German-speaking theatres.

In December, 1997 the Royal Court International Department
has organised a third series of readings of new German plays.
This time we are presenting comedies by young German
writers as part of a *New European Theatre Season* in the
Theatre Upstairs featuring the British premiere production of
Stranger's House by Dea Loher. It is particularly rewarding
that Dea Loher was the first young German writer to visit the
Royal Court as part of the exchange programme. She attended
the summer school, took part in rehearsed readings of two
plays and is now produced by the theatre. During the last four
years, a number of writers and directors have been supported
by the British Council including Jens Hillhjé, the young
dramaturg of the Deutsches Theater (Baracke), who spent
four weeks with us learning about our play development
programme. The Baracke is the home of many inspiring new

writing projects in Berlin, and the exchange with them has never been more dynamic. The international exchange with new German writing continues to resonate within the Royal Court and remains a model for all our international work.

Elyse Dodgson

Head of International Department
and Associate Director
Royal Court Theatre, London
September 1997

Acknowledgements

The Goethe-Institut and the Royal Court Theatre would like to thank the following for all their commitment to this project: the writers, translators, readers, directors and actors who took part in the 1995 *New German Voices* season at the Royal Court; Michael Eberth, former chief dramaturg of the Deutsches Theater Berlin who was instrumental in making the occasion a genuine collaboration of plays and ideas; the British Council who supported the work of the exchange in Germany. We would also like to thank the following individuals: Corinna Brocher, Simon Cole, Stephen Daldry, Henrike Hawkins, Keith Lawrence, Angelika Ludwig, Meredith Oakes, Pierre Politz, Elke Ritt, David Tushingham, Ania Wilder-Mintzer and Graham Whybrow for their ongoing enthusiasm and support.

Introduction

The plays in this volume are more than simply four German plays, they're four plays *about* Germany.

Each one was written during the mid 1990s, a time when the nation itself was very much a work-in-progress. Following the fall of the Berlin Wall in November 1989 and formal German reunification in October 1990, Germans on both sides suddenly found themselves living in a distinctly different place; one with new borders, a new population, new neighbours and new responsibilities. The whole question of national identity – of who is and who isn't German and what being German actually means – acquired a new urgency in the context of a sudden and unexpected marriage between the Democratic and Federal Republics, East and West Germany.

It's this urgency which gives these four plays their dynamism and their life. The sheer persistence with which issues of cultural identity keep thrusting themselves to the fore in these plays is a response on the part of their writers to a situation where no one – writers included – could feel at ease with the notion of who 'we' are.

Such a situation brings with it a whole set of challenges. And for artists it tends to be during uneasy times like these that the rest of society looks to them for help. Each of the four plays that follow takes up that challenge eagerly, and it's interesting just how different the means are with which the individual playwrights have done so.

Klaus Pohl, the oldest and most established of the quartet, responds by forsaking fiction altogether. Pohl didn't invent the characters in *Waiting Room Germany*, he found them, travelling round Germany on a journalistic assignment for *Der Spiegel* magazine. He may have shaped and edited the material but none of it is made up, it's all passed on verbatim, out of the mouths of real people, real Germans.

When I first read the full-length, original-language script of
Waiting Room Germany, I could hardly put it down. Here was
a fascinating sociological document. Yet I had difficulty
imagining it on stage. The text was so long the agent had had
to divide its two hundred plus pages between two separate ring
binders – and was it really a play at all? However, perform-
ances in both Berlin and London have seen the work
triumphantly vindicated. Pohl's front-on presentation of each
character calls for acting of the most ingenuous and concen-
trated nature, while what the characters say can suddenly
hurtle in absurd directions, like the West German insurance
salesman who appears to be obsessed with East Germans' body
odour or the security guard at a political meeting who is afraid
to say he likes beer in case it means the Germans will all be
branded as alcoholics.

The effect is a remarkably potent and pure form of drama, one
that is as faithful to the minutiae of life as it is to the epics,
like the story of Hans, the master painter from Görlitz, and his
career as a victim of the Stasi, the East German secret police.
The fact that we in the audience know the words were spoken
by 'real people' and that the actors we see on stage are also
real people but not the same ones has a curiously positive
function, one which is enhanced by seeing the actors double
more than one role. Watching one actor play two different
people with sharply conflicting opinions suggests that our own
experiences and attitudes may not be as fixed as we assume.
In other circumstances, we could easily have been in someone
else's shoes. As such, a performance of *Waiting Room
Germany* does something that all the best theatre is supposed
to do: it makes us feel we have something in common with
people who were complete strangers.

Anna Langhoff's play *The Table Laid* is full of strangers. Set
in an *Asylantenheim*, a temporary shelter for asylum seekers, it
offers a view of the lives of a group of refugees from countries
to the east who have come to Germany in hope of a better life.
Here the kitchen becomes a vision of eastern Europe in
microcosm, a place where there are too many people and not
enough room, where people mistrust each other because of
cultural differences and misunderstand each other from the

lack of an adequate common language. It is also a vision of
what a multi-cultural Germany might become, a place where
everyone speaks German as a second language, badly, and
Germans, like Frau Mertel, the social worker, are an exotic and
rather intrusive presence. Langhoff makes the point well that
it's traditionally watchful German bureaucracy which initiates
the whole cycle of distrust and aggression – something she
tries to overcome in the audience by appealing directly to the
senses, having each family prepare and cook a national dish on
stage during the performance.

While Anna Langhoff is interested in the ubiquity of the
immigrant experience, in the fact that the sheer volume of
numbers seeking asylum in Germany have turned it into an
issue, Dea Loher prefers to concentrate on one individual
experience. Her play *Stranger's House* shows a single, epic
narrative rather than a bustling milieu. Yanne has run away
from poverty and a looming war in Macedonia and has come
to Germany hoping to stay with his uncle's friend Hristo.
Here, Yanne's encounters with women are filled with an erotic
tension. Those with men are characterized by other tensions
of a less appealing kind. The manner in which Yanne's arrival
turns into the nemesis of both Hristo and his family is told
with lucidity and power. Loher's play deals in hot dramatic
themes like jealousy and betrayal, and its force comes from
the fact that these are handled with unpretentious assurance.
The strength and originality of the play's perspective is evident
in the final scene, when Yanne agrees to marry Nelly, a woman
he does not love, in order to qualify for a residence permit.
Such arrangements tend to be viewed by citizens of the
country concerned in terms of what those involved have to
gain – in Yanne's case, Loher presents the agreement in terms
of what he has to lose. It's a poignant and telling piece of
writing.

The title of the last of the plays, *Jennifer Klemm or Comfort
and Misery of the Last Germans*, is reminiscent of Brecht's
Fears and Miseries of the Third Reich, a revue-like compilation
of short scenes with a clear political message. It is also the
most eclectic and wide-ranging of the pieces in this volume.
However, where Brecht's concerns in the Thirties were

essentially with the moral meltdown in Nazi Germany, Rust's Nineties apocalypse is one beyond politics, manifesting itself in the erosion of reality and of the individual.

Not ending until after the audience have left the auditorium, *Jennifer Klemm* is a splattergun attempt to engage with the accelerating chaos of contemporary living which makes few concessions to established theatrical form or the comfort of those either creating or watching a performance. The world it shows on stage is not a world – it is a series of images. The identities of those we see are not reliable. Even the author's name, D. Rust, sounds impersonal and asexual. It's a postmodern nightmare, staged not in an attempt to elicit an audience's credulity, but to challenge its incredulity.

All four plays in this collection are strong stuff. In confronting recent German history and contributing to one of the world's most radical and dynamic theatre cultures, they have to be. The theatre for which these plays were written may differ from our own in numerous respects, but each one is a concerted effort to make that theatre an important place to be. If that isn't a recommendation, I don't know what is.

David Tushingham

GERMAN PLAYS

Plays from a Changing Country

WAITING ROOM GERMANY

by Klaus Pohl

translated by David Tushingham

Klaus Pohl was born in Rothenburg-ob-der-Tauber in 1952 and now lives in New York. He trained at one of Germany's leading drama schools, the Max Reinhardt-Seminar in Berlin, and has acted in productions by Luc Bondy, Giorgio Strehler, Robert Wilson and many others. He is one of the most performed contemporary German writers. His plays include *Da nahm der Himmell auch die Frau* (1979) *Das alte Land* (1984), which won the Mulheim Playwrights prize, *Der Spegel* (after Gogol) (1986), *Hunsrück* (1987), *Heisses Geld* (1998), *Die schöne Fremde* (1991) and *Karate Billi kehrt zurück* (1991), which premiered at the Deutsches Schauspielhaus in Hamburg followed by productions in 27 other German theatres and as *Karate Billy Comes Home* was performed in the Royal Court Theatre Upstairs in 1992. In 1995 Pohl wrote and directed *Wartesaal Deutschland: Stimmenreich*, which opened on 28 October 1995 at the Deutsches Theater Berlin and has been produced all over Germany. It was first performed in English at the Royal Court Theatre Downstairs on 9 November 1995.

Waiting Room Germany was first performed in English as a rehearsed reading in the *New German Voices* season in the Theatre Upstairs on 3 October 1995 with the following cast:

Susan Brown
Neil Dudgeon
Cherry Morris
Robin Soans
Danny Webb

Director   Mary Peate
Translator   David Tushingham

The British premiere was subsequently staged at the Royal Court Theatre Downstairs, first performance 9 November 1995, with the following cast:

Maureen Beattie
Freda Dowie
Neil Dudgeon
Barry Jackson
Robin Soans

Director   Mary Peate
Translator   David Tushingham
Designer   Stewart Laing
Lighting   Johanna Town
Sound   Paul Arditti

A Note on the Text

Waiting Room Germany is unusually open in form. There is no prescribed cast or order of speeches. It can be performed by one actor, by a cast of thirty, or any number of combinations in between. All the characters are real people speaking their own words, shaped into speeches by the author from personal interviews. The full text is too long to be performed in a single evening. The edition printed here was the one used as the basis for the production at the Royal Court Theatre, London, in November 1995. Anyone planning a production of their own may wish to consult a fuller version, available in English translation from Nick Hern Books, 14 Larden Road, London W3 7ST, or in the original German from Rowohlt Theater Verlag, Hamburger Strasse 17, D-21462 Reinbek, Germany.

4

Characters:

Insurance Man

Press Officer

Politician's Private Secretary

Writer

Taxi Driver

Psychiatrist

Old Woman from Berlin

Mayor of Bebra, *a town in West Germany*

Mayor of Harzgerode, *a town in East German*y

Factory Worker

Professor

Car Mechanic

Engineer

Chief Executive

Frankfurt Christian Democrat

Dissatisfied Worker

Local Reporter, *previously Member of DDR Politburo*

Old Lady from Weimar

Security Guard

Master Painter

Actor

Insurance Man

The first time
oh God
the first time I went across
I'm driving across there
get to the border
the wall was down
and the *Volkspolizei* were giving everyone such a friendly wave
I just had to stop
and tell one of them
I told him:
'I'm going to say something now
which isn't very pleasant
you weren't the one who wouldn't let me go the last time
but you're part of the same system
so I'm telling you
if I had my way now
I'd kick your teeth in.'

Press Officer

One has to ask whether it's really right
that we've basically taken a different system
and forced it on these people.
I don't know how the *Wessis* would have reacted
whether they would have been able to show as much
let's call it endurance
as some of the *Ossis* have had to have.
It's as if the Japanese had invaded West Germany and
    announced
from tomorrow you are under Japanese law
everything you have been doing up until now is irrelevant
whether it's traffic regulations or tax law
even the constitution
forget it!
From tomorrow everything's Japanese!

Politician's Private Secretary

For me more or less everything's changed.
Before I was an academic
I used to sit here at my desk
quietly writing my dissertation
articles books and stuff.
The sort of thing that academics do:
international criminal and civil law.
And I had a husband
and so on and so forth
and we all lived here together
the three of us.
You've got to understand that
the DDR was coming to an end.
Something else was on its way
you could see
it was all going down the drain
with things like banning *Sputnik* magazine.
Then when he left us
at the end of 87
beginning of 88
I really felt:
society's fucked
my relationship's fucked
everything's fucked!
So.
When I told people
we wouldn't make it to the next century
everyone laughed at me.
But there were signs everywhere that things were coming to
    a head.
Then the butter crisis happened
and loads more people left.
Buildings started emptying around you:
another one gone here, another empty window there.
You could feel it in the air:

the End is nigh.
Like you can tell a storm's coming
because the flies keep so close to the ground.
Well.
I flipped.
Everything was suddenly going so fast
one thing being replaced by another
then finally everyone breathed a massive sigh of relief.
We thought a new era was going to begin.
the new DDR!
We were all very shaken by it:
I was ill for three months with a sweat gland abscess
sitting round with icepacks under my arm the whole time
I could only walk like this.
I told people my body was purging itself of socialism.
Everything seemed to be festering away.
It was like: you knew it was all going to come crashing apart
but you had no idea where the break was going to come
and which direction it would take you.
What did come was a huge disappointment.
I didn't want to be part of West Germany.
It was unrecognisable.
Suddenly they were only taking on Westerners:
we were pushed aside overnight.
From planned economy to market economy – bang.
It might work with the economy. But not with people.
The quick fix had irreversible consequences for them.
On 3rd October my job was terminated.
They got rid of me.
Herr Reckers came over from the Chancellor's office
we got certificates
with heartfelt thanks for your contribution to German unity
shake hands *auf Wiedersehen*
hello unemployment.
It was a huge stroke of luck
that I managed to find something else.
What saved me was having such a big gob.
So.
I applied to the regional government in Brandenburg
and they took me on and found me a job.
It would never have happened
if I hadn't had a doctorate.
At that level they normally only take people from the West.
And now I'm Stolpe's Private Secretary.

I do everything for him
and anything Eastern is my job
when people ring up saying they'll hang themselves
or set themselves on fire.
Then we've got to *do* something.
They ring me saying things like:
'If you lot don't do this and that
I'm gonna hang myself right on your doorstep.'
Desperate people.
I get a lot of them.
I make sure I go and see them.
The big problem is that
for the DDR population, which still exists here –
that's the amazing thing:
they've managed to emigrate without going anywhere –
the laws are all different
the punishments, the rules have changed
and none of the poor buggers can see their way through it.
So.
If you're anything like me
I mean I can't face seeing them all cry
then I go and sort it out for them.
And of course the word gets round.
That's what I try to explain to all these officials
who've come over from the West
who don't understand this at all!
They have no idea what's going on here!
They simply don't appreciate the scale of the problem!
The people just get in their way!
I end up shouting at them, telling them
there ought to be a sign up here:
YOU ARE PAID BY LOCAL PEOPLE ALL DAY LONG!
And when those people need you
it's your job to fucking well be there for them!
Not too busy shunting a load of forms
from one side of your desk to the other.
Because that's bollocks!
So.
Two different worlds are colliding head on there.
There was one bloke rang up for example.
Owned a haulage firm quite near here, just outside Berlin.
And this bloke explained
he owned a piece of land
– it's all connected to this issue of

Westerners claiming property in the East –
he's got this land
and he's fought it out so that he can keep it
but he's got this haulage business –
he has horses –
and now he needs to build a stable for them on his property.
But because everything's new
and everything has to be approved again
he needs planning permission
and because right now that's what everyone needs
there are millions of applications piling up
and at the moment there's an 18 month wait
for an application to get processed.
Now the other guy, the *Wessi*,
who still wants the land back
just won't leave him alone.
So.
He's been poisoning the dogs, poisoning the animals
trying to get rid of him
and that means:
the bloke has to have a stable for his horses and his animals
      right now
and if he doesn't get one, then the animals will all be dead
and he won't need a stable any more.
He'll be ruined.
So.
What do you do?
I've got him on the other end of the phone in floods of tears:
'the Prime Minister is my only hope,' he's saying.
That's what they all want:
a few words with the king as it were
but they don't get to speak to the king
because I'm there.
And I ring his local council Chief Executive's office.
You see that's the great advantage
of you doing all the groundwork:
you know everyone.
So I can call the Chief Executive
and say: 'Burkhard. Come on. Stop sitting on the fence!
There's a man in tears here.
Now listen. Find his planning application –
now I know you're not allowed to do this –
but stick it on top of the pile and get it approved quick.
Or else the previous owner is going to kill all his animals.'

'So what's he ringing you for?'

And I say: 'Yes, I wonder.

Probably because you told him to go to the back of the queue.

I know what you're like!'

And then of course I say the Prime Minister has asked
   specially!

In fact he doesn't know the slightest thing about it.

But I do a bit of the old Politburo

making him personally responsible

calling him *du* all the time

and in the East that still works like magic.

And then I had a woman who was really at her wits' end.

Her daughter had been sleeping around.

She'd picked up a gang of Russians and was hanging about
   with them

in their barracks getting up to all sorts

Fourteen or fifteen she was

she'd dropped out

hadn't been to school for over a year.

The mother was quite desperate.

'You know something,' she told me.

'I'm gonna get a can of petrol

and set myself on fire right outside the Prime Minister's office.'

Now there are two reasons you don't want this to happen:

(a) because it's a political issue

people setting fire to themselves outside government offices

and (b) because it is a shame about the woman.

Insurance Man

Plauen, yes:
it's going back a while now
going back
well four years ago
it was just after the wall came down
I went over
to get things established.
One result of opening the border
was that the whole Western health insurance system
came in.
And just then
every insurance company was making a big effort –
it was a fiercely contested market.
Anyway, Plauen.
It was very nice at the beginning.
Of course it meant a lot of hard work
and I wasn't exactly popular
I was the ultimate *Wessi*!
First in in the morning and last to leave.
I used to make them twitch
they would all stand to attention
when I came into the room.
Because I told them:
There's one thing I don't like –
I made it very plain –
this
this er
this vocabulary
they would always come out with
brigades and er
what was it they used to say
I told them:
'We'll have none of that here!
We're in the West now
and we're going to work in a western way.

I'm not your brigadier
and I won't let myself be called that.
We are all employees
and I am the most senior employee' –
sometimes a highly dubious privilege!
My main priority was
not to leave a disaster behind me.
That when the time came for me
to leave Plauen
I could hand it over
in full working order – and it would stay working.
They'll never forget me for that!
And what's happened since
that I'm particularly pleased about
which is a real positive development
is that the Plauen branch
is now run by local people:
they've come that far in this short time.
Two women run it.
They're the managers!
One of them, one of my appointees, is the deputy,
and the other one who's taken it over now
is a particularly intelligent woman
who I always used to have right at the front
where we had our information centre
and I put her there
because she seemed particularly attractive.
She was dark and very striking
and she used to say hello to everyone who came in,
this smart lady at the reception desk,
who is now the manager.
I had to appoint 27 people
together with a certain Herr Schal from Hof
and I picked 26 women
that was my contribution to German reunification:
women only.
The regional office gave me a warning
I dealt with that in one sentence:
What we want are customers
and that depends to a large extent on outward appearances
Women are better-looking than men!
Of course you need to have at least one token man
but I'd already got him.
'That's me!

The token man.'
To begin with we went round the factories
I had to do most of the business myself
visiting companies
they would take one look at my suit and briefcase
and send me straight to the boss
then it all depends
on how you handle the meeting
I say you've got to be able to work with your voice –
it has to resonate
it also needs a comic touch occasionally
they've got to be able to hear: that's alive!
it has to be alive
not just dripping out of your mouth.
The whole occasion
has to be a positive experience.
Another thing I told them –
they couldn't care less
I did –
was the importance
of presentation.
If you give someone
a business card
it has to be clean
not dog-eared
it has to make a mark.
Otherwise the client'll think you're a fool!
And that also means the building has to be clean and tidy.
What always bothered me most
was their toilets.
The pissoir – it was one of the stupidest things.
I told them: I get the impression
everyone misses when they go for a pee.
What actually caused it –
I was never one to mince my words –
what caused it was the flush
whenever you pressed it down – pfffft! –
some of it always squirted out
and the drips
missed the pissoir and landed on the floor.
The pressure was too high.
In the pipes.
So I said: let's lower the pressure
So that's what I did

we ripped out all the old plumbing
and had Western plumbing put in everywhere.
So that the pressure was right.
Some things you've got to say to people straight out.
Mm. No matter how unpleasant or embarrassing. Mm.
One woman used to stink of sweat.
Take more showers.
No.
No-no.
I didn't tell her: You should take more showers.
I said: you should pay more attention to personal hygiene.
I said it to her alone.
Not in front of all the others.
That's the stupidest thing you could possibly do.
Forget that.
Not in front of everyone else.
I had my own office.
That helped.
I got her in and said it to her.
It's purely a question of cultivating good habits.
Personal hygiene consists of showering regularly, washing
    regularly
and not just your face! but all the other embarrassing bits too.
If I change my shirt every day the smell of sweat in my clothes
can never be very strong even if I don't wash very regularly!
But if I wear the same shirt three days a week –
then the smell starts to sink in and broadcast itself
and that reflects badly on the company.
I explained to her,
that if you went up to the cash desk it didn't seem to smell
    very nice.
And then the lady said she understood.
Most of them would come to see me in *my* office.
Mm! It smells of the West. They used to say.
They wanted to come inside.
I would be wearing cologne and that smelt nice,
it created a pleasant atmosphere.
Wherever I went there was always a little bit of a cloud
    hanging around me.
And I made it quite clear to the people in Plauen:
what I do, anyone else can do too.
As long as they're prepared to make the effort.
It all depends on the effort you put in.
People there didn't care about what they were doing.

You'd turn up somewhere and the receptionists would all be
    filing their nails.
Or talking amongst themselves.
The phone would ring and I'd have to ask them to answer it.
They'd say: if they really want something they'll try again!
It was mad!
I sent one of the staff over to the bank.
I told her to fetch the statements.
I thought she was never coming back.
I could have hopped there and back in that time!
I waited an hour! An hour and a half, two hours!
I needed the statements, I wanted to see how things were doing
and I couldn't leave the office before I'd done the returns.
I was responsible for almost all the work outside the branch
and I had people to visit.
I couldn't waste my time just sitting around on my backside.
I looked all over the place for her.
I thought she was never coming back.
By then it's almost noon.
And she turns up with a new haircut!
Yes, she'd been to the hairdressers.
Yes, she'd always been in her work time before.
Well, your hair grows while you're working doesn't it?
That was the answer I got.
That was the difference in attitudes.
They would grumble that I was always putting in 1000%.
'Does the whole place belong to you?'
They couldn't understand that.
'You're only the brigadier.'
And I said. 'I am not a brigadier, I am the branch manager.'
They thought it was a collective
the society was some sort of collective
that's the way they saw it.
They used to, that thinking's gone now.
But at the beginning you had to explain all that.
Now it's more like here.
It's all fitting into place now.

Writer

They'd started this cadet school
two months before Hungary
and they were looking for people
who were good at sport as well as academically and
    politically –
they were intended to become the army élite
and would be trained there.
I was eleven.
My father sent for me while I was playing football
and told me: this is something
you ought to think about
whether you want to do it or not.
You'll be taught how to shoot
you'll be taught how to ride a horse
you'll be taught how to ride a motorbike
you'll be taught everything you need for the army
and you'll have one holiday a year –
and you'll have to appear before a panel
who will give you sporting and academic tests.
But only if that's what you want!
I agreed on the spot!
And he told me: think about it for a few days
don't say yes straight away!
My mother didn't interfere.
So I spent a couple of days thinking about it
and all I could feel was fear that I might not be one
of these 330 superhumans.
A lot of them dropped out though.
The physical tests were quite tough.
I could do them
I was very fit
and I went along quite happily.
Only: five days
before I went I knew
I was making the biggest mistake of my life

Five days before
I went to the theatre
I went to the theatre for the first time
and saw *A Doll's House*
at the Volksbühne in the Luxemburgplatz.
It was *A Doll's House*
I sat there with my mother
and when Nora leaves –
I identified her with my mother –
when Nora suddenly leaves
slamming the door behind her
I had tears rolling down my face and I didn't know why.
And then it occurred to me: everyone's heart has two sides.
One side of you wants to rush off and be an anarchist
and the other side, the other side of your heart, wants to
    feel safe.
And anyone who says their heart has only one of these
    sides
either the anarchist side
or the other side which wants to stay at home
is lying!
So when Nora slammed the door behind her
I thought:
why aren't I allowed to stay with my family
instead of going to cadet school?
I went anyway.
They gave you a track suit
and two days later you got a uniform
just like the Army ones
they were made to measure.
I was four foot ten inches
and that looks really weird
one of those uniforms on a little kid.
The things used to itch like hell.
It was like a prison
there were watchtowers all around
a very high wall
and guards in all the towers
they let us out once
but only
in groups of four
for two hours
on Sunday.
There were combat exercises

alert: American spies in the area near Weissenfels!
And we all had to rush off and find them.
For about a year and a half it was OK.
Then I wrote to my parents:
I want to be a writer.
What am I doing here?
My father wrote back:
people don't become writers because that's what they've
    been trained for
they do it because they know about life –
I've still got that letter –
and he sent me biographical details
of some famous writers
and they were Hemingway,
Faulkner and Maxim Gorky.
They'd been through the school of life.
Graduated from the university of life.
There was no way out.
So then I claimed to be an enemy of the state!
Nothing happened
none of the bastards believed me
I told everyone!
Told them: socialism stinks!
No reaction.
I would make speeches after lights out
about all sorts of things
Capitalism is better!
Adolf Hitler was right!
So was the Catholic Church!
I wanted to break every taboo possible.
My friends just pissed themselves laughing.
They knew why I was doing it all.
Shut up, they said,
let us get some sleep.
The school was closed down in June 1960.
Then the wall came
August 61
it was the holidays
and everyone was talking about how something had to be done
it was always in the paper:
we will no longer tolerate others poaching our workforce
and there was going to be some sort of reaction
but no one really thought everything would be closed off.
On 13th August I woke up about 11 o'clock

about 11 o'clock my mother came running through the flat
    shouting:
At last! At last!
At last what? I asked
At last we've finally shut the door.
I got on the S-Bahn and went to the station at Friedrichstrasse
the place was full of farmers
from the outskirts of Berlin
who wanted to get out that weekend.
They'd got there
to find everything shut
and they were just sitting there with their suitcases
they'd sold everything they had
on the black market
livestock and furniture
and now they knew they were going to have to go back!
They knew they couldn't buy their things back
they couldn't get across either
so they just sat there crying.
I'll never forget that
swarms of people from Friedrichstrasse to the Brandenburg
    Gate.
And they'd understood instinctively
that they were being shut in.
The intellectuals hadn't!
But the farmers had!
They'd come a day too late
but they'd felt it.
Then there was 68.
Prague.
When Sanda and I came back from the coast
on 22nd August 1968
we thought we'd arrive at Friedrichshagen station
and find the whole city at boiling point.
For the first time one socialist country was invading another
and that was a situation where it was really going to go off.
But there was nothing.
Absolute quiet.
The streets were empty.
Public awareness had died.
I fell in love once with a music teacher at school.
She had thick thighs
and used to sit there looking really unhappy.
Now if I write

about my fat music teacher
and it accidentally gets published
then you bastards will all say:
now he's going all conventional so he'll get published
now he's not a dissident any more.
But because I'm a writer I have to write about it
regardless
of whether it's dissident or conventional!
Honecker's stupidity is not the stuff of literature
nor is defining your position towards the state!
If you'd asked Kafka to define his position vis-à-vis the
   Habsburg monarchy
he'd have polished it off in a diary entry.
It's in there:
a.m. swimming lesson
p.m. outbreak of World War I.
Germany is the only place where it's like this
where writers are seen as alternative priests
who are going to tell you what's good, what's right.
That's why
I've kept my mouth shut
since the wall's been opened.
What can I say about it?
It's one subject
where I prefer
to maintain a deafening
deafening
silence.

Taxi Driver

I came over in 1976
76 yeah
the rest of the family were brought across
my father
had been in prison
in Bautzen
and was released
well bought out
in 76.
We applied for exit visas
and followed him.
I was 17 then.
My father was inside for three and a half years
he couldn't handle this schizophrenic situation in the East
any longer.
He'd got to be quite high up
and he'd had to run with the wolves
and a time came when he didn't want to any more.
He'd stayed over in the West
he'd been allowed to travel
and they went and brought him back again
and locked him up
for contacting enemies of the state.
They kept him in Hohenschönhausen for 18 months
on remand
then sent him to Bautzen,
when I was 13.
I was allowed to visit him once.
By then I was 15
it was a meeting of very few words.
When they put him inside
my reaction was angry and defiant
I'd always been good at school
but I went steadily downhill after that
I was in the second year.

I got into arguments with teachers
and
well
things just went on from there.
Then I had to leave for the West.
Even though in the meantime
my life had changed a great deal.
I had a girlfriend.
I was in love
and I didn't want to leave any more.
I wanted to stay there.
In the DDR.
But I was 17
I wasn't an adult
and I had to go
I had no choice!
We were told to pack our bags
it all had to be done in 24 hours.
I said goodbye the day before.
Then we travelled out through Friedrichstrasse.
They wouldn't let us past the checkpoint
till we'd missed our train.
Then I started an apprenticeship
in Munich as a car mechanic.
I thought that would interest me
fiddling around with cars and stuff.
But I wasn't happy at all
I just kept crying all the time
suddenly bursting into tears
because I was so homesick
I couldn't understand what was going on.
I had huge rows with my father
we ripped lumps out of each other.
I told him: I've got to go back.
I dropped out of the course
and went back to Berlin.
I managed to visit my girlfriend a few times
I could get across to see her
until I was 18.
As soon as I was 18
I wasn't allowed over any more.
There was no reason.
They don't give you a reason.
It's perverse.

I wasn't allowed in! End of story!
By that time we'd got engaged in Prague and everything.
But they wouldn't let me back in.
Eventually she broke off the relationship
under pressure from her father
he was under pressure from the State Security.
He was involved in training young people
so they told him if he wasn't even able
to bring up his own daughter properly
and get her to change her ways
then he was hardly in a position
to instruct young citizens of the DDR in the correct way
    of life.
So I was all alone in West Berlin.
We wrote each other over 200 letters.
I've still got most of them.
Then the time came when I told myself:
you've got to forget the whole fucking East.
That's when I started taking drugs
I
I drifted off –
never finished the apprenticeship.
They weren't just soft drugs either.
Really odd things happened to me.
Difficult.
It was the loneliness.
I had a series of brief flings
but there was never any love.
I'd turned her into a goddess
and that makes it hard to find anyone new . . .
I don't remember much about what happened then.
Over the years I kept on trying
to re-establish contact with her
because I felt there was still something there
something I needed to sort out.
I just wanted to see her again
but she never wanted to.
Eventually she did reply
we met up
and it was very nice
we felt really close
even though we'd not seen each other for such a long time
there was a little bit of love left there after all.
Some disappointment too

because
well I realised I didn't find her at all attractive.
That was a bit of a relief too to be honest.
We hadn't seen each other for 13 years.
For me it was tremendously important
that they opened the wall again.
She never got married.
She had a kid some time
with some bloke who'd always fancied her.
I don't see her any more,
sadly.
She lives with a bloke I used to know
an old adversary
he's jealous, he doesn't like her seeing me
because there's still a little bit of love left in her too.
I can't call her.
I can't go round.
She doesn't want me to.
Maybe I was cheated out of part of my life
but I've had other chances
I passed my *Abitur*
and became a student again.
I've been driving a taxi for the last six and a half years
part-time to start with
I began a while back studying art history and ethnology
and this was a way of paying for it
I've not finished it yet –
that's another of these things
not getting that finished –
But I'm still registered for
art history and ethnology:
restoring old railway monuments.
I've been doing it nine years now.
Somehow I don't think it'll ever get finished.

Psychiatrist

We'd be told: The oppressed may now speak
and it would be this petty little voice booming into a
    microphone
'THIS IS THE DDR'
that sort of thing has always been a real German speciality
these divisive concepts
We were always told
that the West was full of capitalists
and the capitalists were shit
and everything that we were guilty of in the recent past
– thank Christ – was their fault
and that meant Hitler, the Nazis and all this German filth
    wasn't so bad
because it didn't have anything to do with us any more.
And since
and since
since then something much better had come our way
and that was
this red fascism
this was an attitude that was forced on you:
that
that
you thought capitalism was the worst thing ever.
I still keep coming up against
this simplistic equation of
capitalism equals imperialism equals
fascism equals concentration camps
in other words
if you're not a capitalist then you can't be an
imperialist and therefore not a fascist or
anything
but if you actually look
at how it all happened
Russia
could not have been more imperialist

while Hitler was around
and then they carried on doing it for another 40 years!
it wasn't until 49 that they really got started!
The redder than red communists
the ones who came back from Moscow
all had this thing
fixed in their skulls about
ideals of human advancement in the modern age
something like that.
Whatever, they had some sort of ideal person in mind
and everyone assumed
that that was what you had to be
and if you weren't like that now
then you better become it quick!
And er
eventually I decided I wasn't playing any more
and I said: I don't care about what you think people ought to
    be like
I'm going to go and join those evil capitalists
and do what I want to do!
It meant you were a total outcast
but what the hell.
I'm going to go
where I'm supposed to belong.
I'd just got out of prison
I was still on probation
you can't risk more than that!
and I got away!
And over here
maybe in certain respects it was just like the DDR but
at least you could choose what to do about it
for the first time you could choose
how you wanted to react to what was on offer
you could choose your profession
and how you wanted to do things.
It was entirely up to you
no one was trying to force you to do a particular job
or whatever!
I'm sure I spent a lot of my time
on thoroughly daft things
but still
it was my own life I was living
You see
when you got out of that cage

that gigantic concentration camp
full of lunatics –
I know what I'm talking about –
And you got out here!
You really could
throw yourself into life
I'm going here now or I'm going there!
Money – amazing!!
I had huge problems with it
for years afterwards
I couldn't handle money
because I hadn't the slightest idea what it was
I didn't realise what it meant
the stuff
you see
I had no real understanding of it.
The money in the East was useless.
It was a joke.
And this sudden feeling
of I can do whatever I like . . .
it was quite daunting
but ultimately it inspired me
THAT THAT'S ME
FOR THE FIRST TIME
I HAD A REAL LUST FOR LIFE
A HUNGER FOR IT
And not just fear
. . . and we've all got
a pretty hefty biography behind us
which is all bound up with this point
that the world's been divided so conveniently
with all the pigs over there
and all the good guys here with us
and eventually
you've got to say
I DON'T WANT TO BE YOUR PIG FOREVER
I'D RATHER GO AND LIVE WITH THE PIGS
then at least I'll be left alone.
And
and they say
alright piss off then
and then suddenly they come trotting along wanting a pension
for being so thick in the first place!
That's the Germans for you!

I'm one of the ones who got out
and I got out
under very difficult
circumstances
I
I
I risked MY LIFE!
So just when you think: right, that's finished
along they all come
and it's always:
WE'VE BEEN SO BADLY TREATED!
JUST 'COS WE'RE THE *OSSIS*!
And all that crap
and
and you can only think
you've not nearly been treated badly enough
you cunts
first you should sort out your own mess
your pavements
your FRIDGE!!!!
and keep your mouths shut!
But instead it's the poor *Ossis*
and the SOLIDARITY LEVY
and money
and unemployment
and Nazis
and suddenly the tables have been turned
and the grotesque face!
eh!
which had been hidden all this time
has finally been revealed.
What's going on? Fascism.
That's what's going on!
Right now everything bad is coming
from over there
honestly!
At least for someone like me
where I think: *You* ought to be paying *me* a pension!
I can't run away again
that would be the second time!
It stinks when someone tells you:
you can kiss my arse for all I care
I don't give a fuck whether you live or die
and you tell them OK and you leave, you go somewhere else

then five minutes later they turn up and ask can you spare a
    few Marks
simply for being stupid enough to talk such shit for years and
    years.
That's great, that is.
How come they're my neighbours?
I don't want them!
They didn't want me
as their neighbour either.
They didn't want me looking them in the face
they couldn't have cared less what happened to me
if they'd held PUBLIC HANGINGS
those people would have gone and watched
me getting my head chopped off.
They would.
I swear to you.

Old Woman from Berlin

Five years ago is it now?
What! It can't be. Dear me. Five years – oh my God!
I must say so much has changed.
We've got all these unemployed people
and we can get all these things that we never had before
and everyone can travel wherever they want.
If they've got the money.
I haven't been anywhere.
Nowhere at all.
I can't, I've got a son at home who's sick,
I have to stay at home,
I can only get as far as the cemetery,
I can't leave him on his own any longer.
The reunification has done nothing for me,
no, not for me, nothing.
But my other two sons, they've both done a lot of travelling.
I don't begrudge them it
after all the hard times they've been through.
We were stuck in Berlin in 45.
We'd been evacuated a couple of times, to Wartegau.
A woman with three children for God's sake!
They didn't want us anywhere . . .
We were stuck here in the cellar and it had all been in vain.
Still, we survived.
I'll never forget the war as long as I live, the things we saw.
A thousand years could go by and I'd still not forget.
The dead soldiers piled up in the Friedrichstrasse, this high
    they were!
And standing on top of the house to put out the fire next door –
you won't forget that! The whole city was in flames!
I have to tell you, I have nothing to do with politics.
That's finished as far as I'm concerned.
I'll be 80 in September, I'm taken care of, let's say,
and as long as I still can
I'm going to do what I can for my son and I.
Politics isn't my responsibility any more.

During the war we would go out with the three boys
and dig roots up out of the snow to make coffee.
Indoors everything froze; the ink, the coffee!
The windows just had thin black paper over them
and it was such a cold winter. But we didn't freeze.
My beautiful homeland. That's what I like most.
All of it. The whole of Germany. Especially the Baltic coast;
Rügen, Warnemunde, Heringsdorf. Stockmunde.
The countryside where I come from,
West Prussia, which is now in Poland, that's very beautiful too.
We'd be so happy when the first flowers appeared,
when the heather was in bloom.
There was a wood behind our house
we used to pick blueberries there by the bucketful,
we had everything, wonderful game, it was gorgeous.
Germany was very, very beautiful in those days.
The people had to work so hard, day and night.
It was called Steinow, the village, and it was very poor,
it really was nothing but stones, but so beautiful.
We used to go and fetch Easter water and all those sorts of
    things.
On Easter Day we used to have to get up very early, before the
    sunrise,
and go down to the spring.
The water came out of the ground, you could see it coming
    out,
icy-cold, beautifully clear and it tasted so good.
We used to put bicarbonate of soda in it;
vinegar, bicarbonate and sugar,
you could go on drinking it till you burst,
my children would have drunk themselves to death on the
    stuff.
It was lovely. You don't get that any more.
I don't want to complain.
The people were different in those days.
At New Year everybody would call out to each other.
Later it got so bad nobody could laugh any more . . .

Mayor of Bebra, a Town in West Germany

What annoyed me most this morning
was the appointment I had with my dentist
which I'd arranged specially for this morning
had to be cancelled
because my crowns weren't ready.
Now here I am without any crowns on my teeth.
You'll have to excuse me if
er
my lip . . .
Here we are in front of the Old Town Hall
in Bebra.
It cost about a million Marks to renovate.
And these hens
you can see along the front:
they're made of concrete.
We got them from Thüringen
from an artist in Thüringen
who makes all sorts of concrete animals:
crocodiles, elephants, hens.
Because the Old Town Hall
was originally a farm
we thought it would be fun to have a row of hens here
and a cockerel in front.
To remind people that it was once a farm.
Will you look at that:
someone's knocked the cockerel's comb off.
That's another piece of vandalism.
They're concrete hens, like I said. The hen set!
If you've got a garden give him a call,
he'll deliver.
But the unification! Reunification!
Complete and total reunification!
When the wall came down
the town of Bebra made 1200 Marks' worth of coffee.
We did it in shifts.

People were getting up at four in the morning
to make coffee for all the people coming from the East
coffee
coffee
coffee
coffee
Now there was no way the town could have predicted the
    reunification
and everything has to be budgeted for in advance
so we just didn't have this 1200 Marks' coffee money for the
    reunification!
It's obvious!
Anyhow the Edeka coffee company volunteered
and said we'll put in 1000 Marks and everyone gave a
    donation.
But the ones
the ones who really made a packet
the supermarkets like Aldi –
they didn't give us a thing!
We were all euphoric about the situation:
the border has gone,
Bebra is slap bang in the middle of Germany,
I'm the Mayor:
things can only get better
with industry coming in and so forth.
Instead the opposite has happened.
The federal authorities have closed their offices down
like customs
and border patrols
there used to be 25 customs officers here
with dogs.
The railway police –
moved to Fulda!
No one in Bebra believed reunification would ever happen.
Why did I become Mayor of Bebra?
Well
personal reasons partly
Bebra is a place where you can keep an eye on everything
but because you can still keep an eye on everything
there are a lot of demands on your time.
Loads of people make appointments
to come and see me.
The usual problem is people
driving too fast.

Another thing that keeps cropping up is
people not getting on with their neighbours
then for some reason
THE MAYOR AS AN INSTITUTION
is supposed to intervene
because they haven't got the guts to go and talk to the people
    next door
and sort it out between themselves.
Their neighbours don't even know that there's a problem:
that at that very moment neighbour number 1
is sitting in the Mayor's office complaining about neighbour
    number 2.
Nowadays we live in a state
which wants everything minutely ordered and regulated
and these regulations bear no relation to what happens in
    practice.
Everything is regulated
down to the tiniest detail.
I'll give you one example.
Of course there are rules for kindergartens.
But there's a rule for the precise distance
between the hooks for the children's coats.
Because it might be possible
for a flea to jump between them.
They've measured it.
The distance has to be
this is of the top of my head
at least 8 cm.
All this gets written down
and enshrined in law.
Another example!
The State of Hessen
and the town of Bebra
are building a cycle path together.
Building in inverted commas that is.
Because they've been doing it for 15 years now
and the thing still hasn't been built yet.
And why is that?
Because the path runs alongside a national park.
It wouldn't actually enter the protected area.
The edge of the cycle path or the edge of the road
would touch the edge of the protected area.
That's all that would happen: they would touch each other.
But for the conservation authorities

that means: NO!
They've used various arguments:
that the animals would be disturbed
if a cyclist stopped to have a look round.
There are grey herons there.
There was a suggestion that
we put the cycle path on the other side of the road.
Even though there are woods there
and it would mean felling the first rows of trees
and that cyclists coming from Bebra
would have to cross the B27 – a very busy road.
So to stop them from being run over and killed
we were supposed to build an underpass.
That underpass would have cost half a million Marks!
And that's where I said:
'Hang on!
It is simply not on
that the life of a frog or a swarm of mosquitoes
or a grey heron –
never mind merely causing them a disturbance –
is going to cost that kind of money!
I won't allow it!'
So then we had a meeting
with a representative
of the Federal Environmental Protection Authority.
He told us all about the grey herons.
'If a cyclist stops on the cycle path
and a grey heron happens to be there
then the grey heron is going to be disturbed.'
So I told him:
'Right, this is what we'll do,
we'll build a screen all round the park.
It doesn't matter what the cyclists do then
they won't ever see any grey herons.'
And that will be the answer.

Mayor of Harzgerode, a Town in East Germany

I was Mayor of Harzgerode
for ten years
between 1980 and 1990.
I stopped on 15th March 1990
I stood down officially
and handed over
all my official duties.
It was all done properly
and initially
after a lot of thought
I decided to distance myself
quite firmly
from all party-political activities.
At that time
I felt very badly let down
by our SED
I have to say that
I'd spent my entire life
doing a great deal for the Party
I was quite aware of what I was doing
and I genuinely supported the ideals
which the Party used to stand for.
I come from a pure working-class background
I trained as a carpenter
before changing jobs
that's when I came here to Harzgerode
there was industry here
die-casting it was then
a small company
and the company then chose me to go on a course
and I studied economic management for five years.
Five years of evening classes
working during the day and studying at night
and on top of that
in my spare time

I was a musician in a dance band
trumpet
I played.
I was an economist
in the labour department.
Then I was put in charge
of personnel, training and social welfare.
And then well
in 1980
I had to
I was forced to volunteer
it was well-known
the Party didn't let you discuss these things
the regional First Secretary came along
together with the Council Leader for the area
and they didn't beat about the bush.
Look, Manfred, Comrade,
we expect you etcetera etcetera
will take over as Mayor on 1st October
and if you have any objections and want to get into any
    discussions
we'll be forced to look into your position
vis-à-vis the Party.
You know the town's in trouble
and we expect you
yeah well.
We sat down and had a meal
with the Council Leader and my predecessor
and the next morning
I took over.
I had a lot of trouble at the beginning
with public speaking
that wasn't easy
and
other problems
getting housebuilding programmes finished
or food supplies
that was one of the biggest problems
we used to have in the DDR.
When the Mayor had to go off himself
to make sure there would be cheese in the shops
I don't even want to think about it
er
every fortnight

there would be these
Supply Commissions they were called
for the whole area.
And it was always about fruit and veg
and one of the things was sliced cheese.
Massive rows every time
I remember I'd made a big fuss
about how there was no cheese in Harzgerode.
And then the Chairman says:
But Manfred!
What the hell do you want!
I've got the list right in front of me!
Only last week you got 6 kilos of cheese for Harzgerode.
6 kilos!
6 kilos!
For a whole town!
That was what made those years
so terribly stressful.
The biggest disappointment for me
is that a well-ordered society
could collapse like that
as a result of so many subjective errors
and I have to keep saying this
that the principal errors happened within the Party.
That's what disappointed me most of all
because the social structure
was designed for the workers
and it was a good system
and the whole of this well-structured society
just collapsed.
And now!
Five years on!
What can I say about this town:
the town's finished!
Harzgerode has got forty per cent unemployment.
The people who were cursing us five years ago
denouncing us
have failed completely.
And now the situation is so difficult
and the demands on myself are so great
that yesterday I submitted nomination papers
and am going to stand
for Mayor of Harzgerode.
In Harzgerode we've had nothing

out of the wall coming down.
Except an Aldi
and that was a struggle.
The place is crippled.
There's nothing going on any more.
Harzgerode used to be
the main town in the Quedlingburg area.
And now we have to be ashamed of ourselves.
If I'm elected:
I can use all the experience I've got
from being Mayor for ten years of the DDR
I can use that again now.
In community politics.
Because in the DDR
we were good at community politics.
Here under this lime tree
is where I negotiated
the rebuilding of our school
with the chairman
of the planning authority.
It was January it was very cold
and we had an extra, private meeting
just the two of us
and I made him change his mind
the school had to be in Harzgerode after all.
My wife knows what I'm like.
She knows if I do it,
then it will go way beyond
what can be expected of honorary office
and she won't be seeing very much of me.
I'll be off early in the morning
and won't be back till late at night.
It's always been my greatest love
this town
and the people here
and that's a love I've never lost.

Factory Worker

I make the airbags
well just the parts
for the car airbags
the boss fetches them
and we clean them
cut off bits of waste
check them for holes
or blisters
and then they get soldered
it's a big business
I trained as a confectioner
nougat
we made nougat
for the West
nougat
it used to be exported to West Germany
our nougat
they used to sell it cheap over there
at Christmas time
and people would send it back to us
as Christmas presents
we always used to get
some of our nougat
from our Auntie in Rottweil
that's what used to happen
and we liked that
now I make airbags.

Professor

There's been such an extreme transformation
and so many changes
for me personally!
Well
I'll start at the beginning
For me it had always been a balancing act
between being afraid and toeing the line and a sort of
    measured er er criticism
especially when it came to political psychology
there were a couple of incidents
but they were much too tame
and other people were far braver
just among my closest friends
during that time I made a suggestion
that we set up a course in political psychology
I wrote a working paper
which was discussed here at the university
and as a result of this working paper
I was summoned to Berlin
in April 89
to the Central Committee building
it was the first time I'd been inside
it had these huge long corridors
and something happened there
which hurt me
very deeply
Five people sat in a row opposite me
shouting at me
trying to get me to change my mind
they wanted me to go to Leipzig
and teach a different subject
they wanted me out of social psychology here
and tried to tempt me by saying:
you can do political psychology there
as part of this related discipline

I knew
they wanted me away from this place
that was the main thing
I was still in the SED
and they had these Party commands
you couldn't refuse a command from the Party it wasn't done
I
when I did turn this down I said:
my wife is very ill
my wife
my wife at that time had er
a heart condition
she really wasn't well
I told them
that because I'd gone to Jena in 87
and she didn't want to come too
there'd already been a lot of trouble
because I'd been working very hard
it had caused a great deal of friction
I was very attached to my daughters
and I'd always spent a lot of time caring for them
though mainly at weekends
and if I now had to go to Leipzig
she definitely wouldn't go with me
and the marriage would break up
I didn't want that to happen
we had –
alright
maybe I was too jealous
I'd seen a lot which perhaps wasn't there
but I was simply afraid
of the marriage breaking up.
But they put me under such enormous pressure
also because of this working paper
that I
this is what really hurt me
that I cried in the presence of these four or five men
that they could cut me down so small
really hurt me.
They said: right,
you're going to have another think about this
because no one disobeys a Party command!
And we'll discuss it once more
when your wife is well again

if not before.
Then came the Summer of 89
lots of people left the DDR
and a great deal happened
my best friend
Jakob in Berlin
was already in the opposition movement
and he told me: the time has come when we've got to do
    something.
I told him I was far too afraid
afraid for myself
afraid for my family
afraid for my job
but I'd started having real doubts
when so many people left the country.
Part of me was annoyed by them too.
I thought: why can't you stay here do something here!
Then in September I got ready
to go to Munich for a conference
on applied psychology.
The conference was at the beginning of October
from the 4th to the 10th of October 1989
in Munich
and we visited friends there too
a colleague a psychiatrist
we went to her house.
She said: let's eat later
first we've got to watch the news.
Afterwards she asked. 'How do you feel?
You can stay here if you want to.'
I told her: 'Now I really do have to go back!'
And . . .
yes we went back again
on the thirteenth
the Friday
I went to Berlin
I remember I went to my friend Jakob's house first
had a cup of coffee with him and a cigarette
I was shaking!
He said. 'Hey, what are you shaking for, man?
It's all over. It's finished. There's no need
to be afraid any more.'
I was still very nervous when I went along.
This time there were only two of them.

But it was very tough.
That conversation.
And very hurtful.
With all the old threats.
They still wanted me to go to Leipzig!
And all about my political psychology
and my visit to Munich.
I had to tell them everything that had happened in Munich.
Their manner was extremely unpleasant.
Right, they said, if you won't go to Leipzig
you'll not get a moment's peace in Jena.
That could have meant that
I would lose my job.
And because I'm anything but the resistant type
I have a nervous disposition
when they started using these sort of terms
I got very scared.
That was Friday the 13th!
By ten o'clock at night
I was back in Erfurt.
And my wife came out with:
'I'm sorry. That's it.'
And so the smaller family broke up too.
'It's no use,' she said.
'We can't go on.'
'You've been working so hard you never had any time.'
That's what she said. I didn't believe her.
Until I discovered that what I'd always thought was true.
Her present boyfriend
is the man who was her boss
he's 15 years older than her
more paternal
calmer
not as disorganised!
My whole world was falling apart.
I went mad
driving all over
the south of the DDR
in my Trabi
looking up friends
telling them what had happened to me.
I started smoking again
I've been doing it ever since
by mid-December I'd almost reached the point of saying:

What is there left?
What more do I want?
Everything was falling apart.
The family had collapsed.
How are you going to get yourself out of this hole?
Your ideas, your ideals, are all falling apart!
Despite all this
I have to say
as well as this manic-depressive cycle
there were also moments which were very different
driving here from Erfurt in the mornings
along the empty motorway:
Now you can think
things you've never been allowed to think before!
How many ideas were wrecked here by this institute!
Now you can do anything.
You can think and speak your mind.
And then the mood swung back again.
At the beginning of 1990
the restructuring proposals arrived
and of course I was worried
would I manage to make the jump?
Would I be accepted into the University?
How did I stand?
Well.
At least I've been able to carry on working.
I can say what I did
and I can also say when I was afraid.
I can breathe again.
I can go walking in the woods again.
No. I don't feel I've been punished.

Car Mechanic

I had this ladder outside
the doorway weren't finished
a big steep ladder
a wooden one
like a chicken ladder
and there were a knock at the kitchen here
I thought it were the ladder, it were always banging
but this lad were standing here
and he tells us
he's from one of these
no no
he dun't say nowt
he had a piece of paper
with it written down
that he cun't talk
that he's just learning to speak
he were trying to sell stuff
sponges
he had all sorts of identification
to show he were allowed to sell this stuff
from one of them factories they have for the handicapped
where they make things
and we bought a couple of sponges
13 Marks I paid him
you can get them in the shops for like three.
Ten of these glittery sponges there were
we thought we'd take one
we wun't send him away empty handed
so we got the sponges
and we still use them
come to think of it I think they cost more
we paid 14 Marks
well after that we said
if another one comes along
we'll chuck him down the stairs.

In Schwallungen recently
just recently
this bloke in a wheelchair
went round various people
one of them were the dentist
and he asks the dentist for a donation
because they've got money now those medical people
the dentist give him 20 or 30 Marks
and he made a right fuss
that it wun't enough
and he goes off in his wheelchair
next minute he stands up
walks over to a car
puts the wheelchair in the back
and drives off.
That were a month ago!
Fact!
Stood up, walked away and put his wheelchair in the boot!
All sorts of things go on!
In Wasungen
people come round
and we dun't have these things
little spyholes
in the front door
to look through
and one of these firms or some bloke
went round the flats
telling people
we're doing these spyholes
drilled holes in all their doors
took their money
and disappeared
he never come back.
Everyone got an hole in their door
and that were it.
Or these Italians
in cars
with leather jackets inside
there were
there were a big row here
we were outside in the yard
me and Fritz from next door
we were building a wall
working with cement

in summer
bare chests
and this car stops
a very respectable
middle-aged bloke
well dressed
in a jacket and tie
with all these leather jackets inside
and he asks us
we were standing there
bare chests
like I said
sweat pouring off us
and he tells us
he's just come from this trade fair
he's got to go back to Holland
and he dun't wanna take this stuff back with him
so he's gonna sell 'em off now dead cheap
leather jackets
they were so expensive here
and all that
so Fritz goes and says
er – I might be able to take one
and he tries one on
it were miles too big for him
but he's stood there
I can see him now trying to make it fit
hunching his shoulders.
Oh that fits
if you put something on underneath
that'll fit fine
and then he goes and asks me
I told him if you wanna buy it that's your business.
How much is it then?
two hundred and fifty Marks
it's giving them away
so he goes in the house and gets two hundred and fifty Marks.
He never wears it
that jacket
must be at least three sizes too big.
When Cornelia come home
and he'd spent the last money they had
on that jacket
there were some row.

And that's the thing.
You never used to get conned like that before.
No one was trying to rip you off
it just din't happen
and then suddenly it did.
Well.
The countryside's the same as before.

Engineer

The shift to the right is definitely there but I hope it's getting stuck in its tracks. I haven't seen so much of it here because I live further out in one of the new estates. But you do notice it in certain places in Berlin. Certain people that you see. No, no one's had a go at me yet. But it happened to my husband. Just after the wall came down. Somebody thought he looked Jewish because he had one of those caps on. He's not a Jew, he just happened to have one of these caps on. Wherever it was somebody decided they were going to pick him out for being Jewish and then they attacked him. Things like that happen for no reason. He reported it.

He had a broken rib, various injuries, bruises and things, and it's had other effects too. He's been a bit frightened ever since. They shouted at him: you're a Jew! By the time words had been said on both sides he was on the floor. And what's so hard to understand about it is: there were people there, he called for help and no one did anything. It didn't used to be like that. We had a community and it felt safer.

Chief Executive
(previously Politician in West Germany)

Well
I always say
let's not talk about the past
reunification is irreversible
you can be delighted you can be outraged
no one's really bothered
so let's get on with putting the pieces back together!
These people need something to do.
They're happy when they have something.
And there's so much that needs to be done.
The key moment for me
was when I'd first come here
to Jena
and we had to make 16,000 people redundant
and I saw the old factories
where five people were carrying on pottering about
as if nothing had happened
and I told my people then
I've only just realised
we have to demolish these buildings
otherwise we'll have a disaster on our hands.
There'll be a handful of people in each room
fiddling away at something
and nothing will ever come of it.
We've got to act now
so that we can say:
the people have gone
the buildings have gone
now we need to rebuild
develop something new
something entirely different!
And when the people stood there
watching
us demolish the old factories in the city centre

and they said:
we survived the First World War and the Second World War
but we won't survive Späth
no
he's knocking everything down
I know
I almost cried too.
There was an old man by the gates
watching the big metal ball
smash through the walls on the fourth floor
and he said
I spent 30 years there
polishing lenses
the most beautiful lenses in the world
and he's knocking it all down!
So I went over and told him
I'm the one
who decided to knock that down
and he sort of apologised to me
and said
I wouldn't have said that so loud
if I'd known
you were standing right next to me.
I told him
that's quite alright you say what you like
to be honest
I feel very bad about doing this
but I know
that it's useless
if I start crying about the lenses too
because no one buys them any more.
We have to build a shopping centre
or something like that
because now all the lenses get made in China.
Ah.
OK.
The man
was grateful
that I'd talked to him
we parted very amicably
but I'm sure he went away
shaking his head saying:
THIS HAS GOT TO BE THE END OF THE WORLD.

Frankfurt Christian Democrat and a Dissatisfied Worker

CHRISTIAN DEMOCRAT. What I like most about us in Germany is we've got certain principles of government and economic principles here which are worth maintaining, er what I mean is the er social market economy.

WORKER. If only we'd still got one! Kohl's completely destroyed it in the last ten years.

CHRISTIAN DEMOCRAT. Really.

WORKER. You've scrapped it, scrapped it in a thoroughly anti-social way.

CHRISTIAN DEMOCRAT. Who has? Who?

WORKER. You have. That Kohl government of yours.

CHRISTIAN DEMOCRAT. I'm not in the Kohl government. I voted for them!

WORKER. You voted for them. That makes you responsible for the whole mess.

CHRISTIAN DEMOCRAT. Who did you vote for? If you say I'm responsible. Who did you vote for!

WORKER. The man calls himself Adenauer's –

CHRISTIAN DEMOCRAT. Who was it! Who did you vote for! Who did you vote for!!

WORKER. Adenauer's –

CHRISTIAN DEMOCRAT. WHO DID YOU VOTE FOR!!

WORKER. Konrad Adenauer's grandson!

CHRISTIAN DEMOCRAT. WHO DID YOU VOTE FOR!!

WORKER. Do you know what Konrad Adenauer's greatest achievement was?

CHRISTIAN DEMOCRAT. Who did you vote for!!

WORKER. A state based on social justice. And you destroyed it.

CHRISTIAN DEMOCRAT. Who did you vote for! Stand by what you voted for.

WORKER. In the last parliamentary election?

CHRISTIAN DEMOCRAT. Yes?

WORKER. The party you'd probably find least er acceptable.

CHRISTIAN DEMOCRAT. Just say it.

WORKER. No. Look. I voted for the SPD and the Greens. I split my vote because er well looking at it the other way there really isn't a party for workers to vote for in this state any more. To be perfectly frank all the parties

CHRISTIAN DEMOCRAT. You have no real understanding.

WORKER. I understand alright.

CHRISTIAN DEMOCRAT. No, you don't understand.

WORKER. I understand right enough! I can see what you've done to our health system! I can see what you've done with our pensions! How you're financing the supposed reconstruction of the East! The poor people are the ones who have to pay! It's always the poor people!

CHRISTIAN DEMOCRAT. Everyone pays! Not just the poor!

WORKER. Solidarity levies mean we pay, the working man! It's obvious!

CHRISTIAN DEMOCRAT. No, it's not like that!

WORKER. Solidarity means the working man.

CHRISTIAN DEMOCRAT. Everyone pays!

WORKER. No they don't! The workers are the ones who are paying.

CHRISTIAN DEMOCRAT. Everyone does!

WORKER. We do, the working people. Whether it's unemployment benefit! Or pension or health insurance! The largest single expense a working man has in a city like Frankfurt is rent! And you have the most anti-social housing policy any federal government has ever had. How many homes are you going to build!

CHRISTIAN DEMOCRAT. You don't have to shout. The words mean exactly the same. The louder you shout the less I can hear you.

WORKER. You're cutting back on nursery places. You have to be dying now to qualify for a prescription!

CHRISTIAN DEMOCRAT. We all have to make sacrifices. Every one of us!

WORKER. That would be a fine thing. If you really did mean everyone. For me that means someone who earns a lot pays more than someone who doesn't. And that isn't a special solidarity levy! Then it gets paid for out of taxes...

CHRISTIAN DEMOCRAT. Alright, but I'm sure you're not really paying all that much! Not so much that it justifies this huge palaver! I'm sure every month you spend two or three times as much money on things that at the end of the month you know you spent it but you've no idea where the money went. And you're in exactly the same position as a lot of other people I know: they've got money for Coca-Cola, they eat at McDonalds, for all I know they go to prostitutes and the reason they never have any money is because they spend it on the wrong things.

WORKER. Prostitutes? Well, I can assure you. That is not true in my case.

CHRISTIAN DEMOCRAT. The reason you don't have any money is because you spend it on the wrong things.

WORKER. No!

CHRISTIAN DEMOCRAT. No!! You don't have any money because you spend it on the wrong things!!

Local Reporter
(Previously Member of DDR Politburo)

It's all been gone over so often now
all been said
supposedly. This stuff about I got a memo
that evening: 'Günter. Open the border.'
and so forth, load of rubbish
er
because the memo
there didn't need to be a memo
because
we had the say
in those days
we took the decision
I was one of the three
who deposed Honecker
that's right
we had the say
Well. That's all in the past.
This is where I am now.
As I was saying
I've had the good fortune
to get out of that armour-plated ideology
to escape
those ties are very strong
and this is where I've landed
it's a local paper, run purely on advertising
in Nordhessen
near the old border
on the western side
I have to earn money I have to support my family
who as I was saying are still in Berlin
and this was a chance
otherwise
I didn't have a chance
the paper can only exist

as a free sheet
so we stick to what's going on locally
being a local paper means
we have to stick to local matters.
Right
what is it about Germany
I like most
well
to be quite honest I've got to say
that's a question
that I don't really have much sympathy for
yes well
well
that was never important to me
when I talk about Germany
I can only think of this Germany
the single Germany
that exists now
for me basically
it's never been so much a question of Germany
and the Germans
for me
and the influence is obvious
the main question
has always been the system
Germany my God Germany
that's always been a dodgy idea
when you look at the workers' movement
then
the workers
er
they were always an international movement
that was their great strength
nationalism was Bismarck
nationalism was spiked helmets
the police
the nationalists were bourgeois
little domestic tyrants.
The workers didn't live in beautiful countryside
they were in dark holes
staying in rented rooms
they were never able to cultivate
this feeling of *Heimat*,
this sentimental attachment to the countryside.

It wasn't Germany that I was looking for
when I came here to this little paper
I wanted to understand this other, more durable system
though
for the first time in my life
I drove
in every possible direction
to Bavaria to Hamburg
all over the place
and then
a grandeur
which I had never really been aware of before
which was this idea of *Heimat*
suddenly began to mean something to me
I actually caught myself feeling it
driving through these places
I began to understand why
people do feel an affinity for these landscapes
well to a certain extent I've
driven it out of myself
driven through that
and out the other side
though of course I've always had a soft spot
for Brandenburg
but that was quite
er
er
practical
so
it wasn't so much a beautiful landscape that I saw as:
'It's nice to have a lake here so people can go swimming.'
That's typical of this kind of utilitarian thinking
which divides the world into
useful
non-useful
essential
non-essential
and here I came up against a different way of thinking:
that existence is its own justification
that's something I only really understood here
all that messing around with projections
the plan says this
this must be achieved
by a particular time

and all the stress that followed
because it never was achieved on time
and we used to have to change the plan again afterwards
to make it fit.
That was a real eye-opener for me.
So then I started reading
and this has been one of the most shaming discoveries I've
    ever made
that everything I'm starting to piece together now
things I'm gradually coming to recognise as weaknesses
the causes of our failure
had been known 30 years ago
and all the details written down
I'm the kind of person
who can be profoundly affected by literature
so Koestler
Darkness at Noon
had the hairs standing up on the back of my neck
reading that did.
It shows the way that kind of ideology
destroys people's minds.
That's the drama
the crime
if you want to call it that –
but it's also
a human drama!
We never set out
to be criminals.
Even a man like Honecker isn't a criminal
he was a limited person
a fanatical worker
a proletarian
who tried to change something
though
with a narrowness
which was characteristic of his type.
As critical of him
as I am
I find it very difficult to see what he did
as a crime.
I think it's a dreadful error, a horrendous mistake,
though that offers little comfort to those who were affected.

Old Lady from Weimar

Oh this is the most beautiful country
and I like everything about it
it's all wonderful
I always look on the bright side
and I've been thrilled by the way we've been making up for all
    that time
that was er
I have to say er
it was er
er well!
The top people! They've all been here!
The things we did in the years
when everything was in ruins
I am from Weimar
but I came here originally from Frankfurt
yes I'm very pleased, very pleased
yes
yes
only the escalators go a bit fast
they're too fast for an old woman.
What I like most are the writers.
The best ones are all dead.
My favourite is
er er
Faust!
Our highest achievement.
Faust!
The Prologue in Heaven.

Die Sonne tönt nach alter Weise
In Brudersphären Wettgesang,
Und ihre vorgeschriebne Reise
Vollendet sie mit Donnerklang.
Ihr Anblick gibt den Engeln Stärke,
Wenn keiner sie ergründen mag;

Die unbegreiflich hohen Werke
Sind herrlich wie am ersten Tag.

Do you know *Faust*?

Security Guard

Germany?
What I love
about Germany?
Love?
That's a difficult question.
Too difficult
it might be misinterpreted
if I say beer
er
that what I like most about Germany is the beer
that's er
my er
favourite
you see if I say beer
then someone might get the idea
all the Germans are alcoholics
and that's why er
I'd have to think about it
but just like off the cuff
here
no
I've got work to do!

Master Painter

Over the other side of the Neisse
that's where I was born
in Prager Strasse
I don't get any dole money
or a pension
because I missed so many years
now
I'm stuck here with no money
I'm behind with the electricity
and the rent.
By the end of the month
it could be that I'm out on the streets
dunno where I'd go
I got rehabilitated two and a half months ago
I spent five years inside in the DDR
just 'cos I wanted to go
from Germany to Germany.
I was born here in Görlitz
in 33
did an apprenticeship as a painter
and when I'd done me training
the boss said: 'Sorry, but I can't
pay you fully qualified.'
It was just after the war
that lasted about five months
then I was conscripted to go to Wismut
uranium mine
aye
that's where I worked
the conditions were very primitive
they had none of them underground train things
if a load tipped over
you had to get your back behind it
and right it again yourself
it was terrible

I wanted to get out of there
aye
I did too
got over the border
to the West
near Hof
that was the beginning of 1950
and I got down as far as Nürnberg.
According to Eastern law I was of age at 18
but according to Western law I wouldn't till I was 21
so the first thing they did over there in West Germany
was lock us up
for not having valid papers
and crossing the border illegally.
That meant the West officially recognised
the border with the Eastern zone.
Yeah and they stuck us in a youth home
then one day
they shoved us back over the border
in Sonneberg
in the *Stasi* prison
one interrogation after another
'Why did you come back over?'
'They sent you.'
'You're a Western spy!'
'You're an agent for American intelligence!'
aye
that was how the whole thing started
I tried to escape again
through Czechoslovakia this time
and the Czechs caught us at the border
and they took me down to Joachimstal
and put us in the Czech *Stasi* prison
which was a bit more decent than the German ones
aye
I had to spend six weeks working in a porcelain factory
once I'd done my six weeks
I was tried
sentenced again
this time to six months
for crossing the border illegally
aye
when those six months were up
I was put on a transport

over the border back to Aue
and into the hands of the State Security Service.
And they
the first thing they did
was give us a right doing over
It was the first time I'd ever been seriously beaten up
they used their hands
they used their fists
ha ha
they treated us like scum
kicked me here there.
So then I tried to escape again
like a cat I climbed
right up the inside the light well
in no time I'm on the roof
and over the wall
and by coincidence I met someone
I'd used to work with
I said: you've got to help us out.
Yeah, what is it?
I said the *Stasi* had been keeping us locked up.
I'd got out
and I needed some cash
alright, he says,
I'll help you
I'll meet you back here in two hours' time
and he went straight to the police
escaped prisoner
and all this
I went back to meet him two hours later
police
back inside
kept us in the dark this time
five months in the cells
with the *Stasi*
worn down day and night
in the end I
signed everything
they put in front of me
just so they would leave us alone
then I had time to start wondering
what have I gone and signed now?
Did I just sign my own death sentence?
So I went on hunger strike.

Aye
on the second day
the officer came down
who'd interrogated us
the prisoners called him 'Rat-ear'
he was a nasty piece of work, a right bastard
Stasi Major he was
a bullet had grazed the side of his head
and left him with just the one ear.
He came down to my cell
'Why aren't you eating?'
the guard was there
with a big aluminium bowl.
When I told him: I'm not eating
he still brought the bowl in
boiling hot it was
I picked the bowl up
and threw it straight in his face
it went all over his uniform.
He screamed
'You wait, you pig.
I'll get you for that.
You won't forget this in a hurry.'
He was shouting, wiping the soup off his face.
About an hour later
two guards came down and got us
blindfolded us
and made us crawl up the stairs on all fours
I said I want to withdraw my statement!
You can't withdraw anything
the sentence has already been passed.
'Strip.'
It was the middle of winter
the cell was roughly so high
and there was a wall
I had to climb over the wall
and I wondered what's going to happen now.
Door shut.
And I could hear running water
they'd turned the water on from outside
it started getting higher and higher
and when the water got as high as the wall
I was standing there up to my chest in this icy liquid.
I kept tight hold of that wall

and kept swapping my weight from one leg to the other
so I didn't collapse
with exhaustion
I was really scared
I thought I would drown
in this horrible stuff.
In the morning
around eight
the water suddenly went away
they let it drain off
took us outside
gave us a hot shower
clothes on
then I was taken to Chemnitz
to a normal prison
yeah it was February 51
when I was sentenced.
Prosecutor Bauch
he was big in the Party
gold Party badge
complete bastard
the stuff
he came out with
in his summing up he said:
'Nothing can be proved against the accused
he has only been suspected of these crimes
I would recommend six years' imprisonment
and five years' punishment in the community!'
My collar practically burst
I jumped to my feet
and said
Prosecutor! can you open the window
and let a little justice in here.
Nothing proved and six years in prison in the same breath?
They could twist everything round any way they wanted
it wasn't a public hearing
it was a schoolroom
rows of benches
and a long table at the front
with a smaller table in front of it
where I sat
it was obvious
there was no practical solution
I'd been marked down

the verdict had been fixed before it all began
and then there was someone from the trade union
addressed us
'You're one of a large family. All workers. How could you do
    this to our state! Our workers' and peasants' state! To your
    own family!'
I said what's that got to do with it?
I wanted to go from Germany to Germany!
'You can't say that. We are a separate, independent state.' Blah
    blah blah.
Aye
I was put on a transport to Waldheim.
To start with I was in solitary
then after a few weeks I was put in a cell with three others
four men in a cell for one
shit bucket in the corner
aye
from 51 to January 56 I was in Waldheim
and then I was put on another transport
to Hohenschönhausen
in East Berlin
it was a work camp for the Ministry of State Security
the food was very good
we were allowed to grow our hair again there
and we were given cigarettes
aye
then one day
on the building site
in 56
it was midday
we'd just sat down to eat
and a lorry came to fetch us
numbered roll call
fourteen were released that day
and I was the last one on the list
the night before I'd had a dream
I'd seen exactly what would happen
an officer comes with a list
calls out the names
and one of them's mine.
Hans they're letting you out today!
Rubbish, I said!
I've got another 14 months to do yet!
But it was true.

Went in
had a medical
showered
then we got civvies
they didn't have a jacket that would fit
so I got a ladies' jacket that had been altered
a blue one
with blue Army trousers
and a woollen scarf
an old Russian greatcoat
and one of those poodle caps
with those big flaps over the ears.
When you come out
in Rummelsburg
there's a big open square
at the other end of this open square
is the underground station
there was a train just pulling in
I jumped on
I'd had a quick look to check
it was going to West Berlin
and I sat there
really nervous
there was an old man sitting opposite
he said:
You're from the East aren't you?
From prison?
Have you escaped?
I told him, yes.
He said: get off at the next station
you're in West Berlin
and I managed to get off
without anyone noticing.
I came to a baker's
and I could see the windows were full
of cakes and gateau
and I couldn't stop myself
I just stood there in front of it all and cried.
Eventually I went in with my fifty EastMarks
and said I'd like a couple of slices of cake please
she sees my money and says:
'I'm sorry
we don't take Eastern money here.
But what sort of state are you in?

Where've you come from?'
I've just got out of prison
'You poor thing, come in here'
and she took us into the kitchen
and she gave us a cup of coffee
and a big plate of cake
and told me: 'Eat it, silly, as much as you want,
as much as you can get down you.'
She made sure I was properly fed.
I went to the circus next
Circus Busch
in the West
I went in there
and asked if they had any work.
Yes, if you've got Western papers.
Have you got a trade?
I say I'm a painter and I can do other stuff too.
He said: sorry
not if you haven't got Western papers.
Otherwise I'd take you on right now.
Aye
on the other side of the street there's a police station
passport police
and of course their jaws just dropped
I said: what should I do now
they took us by bus to the airport
and flew us straight out
er
to er
West Germany
and we landed in Hannover
from Hannover they took us to Ülzen
to a camp
there was a medical examination
I was seventy per cent unfit for work
I had a severe heart disorder
stomach ulcers
light tuberculosis
and problems with my circulation.
I got my first Western identity card there
800 Marks to keep us going
and I went to Hamburg.
I'd met a girl in the refugee camp
she was from Hamburg originally

and we got married on 31st December 1956
everyone told us
it's a New Year prank
it'll never work
and one day I had a seizure
she'd told us she was in a special condition
she was pregnant
and I'd been so happy
until it turns out
it wasn't my child
and then she had an abortion
I screamed like a madman
after that I met another woman
and soon after the divorce I married her
and at that time there was a real campaign in Hamburg
you refugees from the East get everything
and we good people of Hamburg get nothing.
The Hamburg people were so envious
it made us ill.
So my wife and I emigrated
let's do something else I said
with a bit of work we'll be OK
aye
I went to Australia
on the MS Aurelia
sick as a dog all the way.
I spent 30 years in Australia
working as a painter
aye
then we saw the wall on television
the uprisings there were here
in Hungary, Poland, all over
we saw them on television.
Right, I told myself,
now it's time to go back to Germany.
I've not seen my mother in more than 40 years
so now I'll go over and see what's up
there's bound to be work
bound to be some way of earning money
so on 19th February 1990
I came back to Görlitz
and my mother
she's already 85.
I said: there's got to be something to do here.

So I went self-employed
I had adverts running in all the local papers for six months
and I got work
it came from all sides
at first on my own
then I had one man
then three
five
and in May last year I was employing 12 people.
Then suddenly the bank foreclosed on us
credit stopped
accounts frozen
because I was owed so much I couldn't continue
and I'd only been paying net wages
there was tax and insurance
and some materials hadn't been paid for.
Now I'm still owed 40,000 Marks
and I can't get it back.
My firm's bust.
And here I am.

Actor

Er
it's
it's
it's
personal
er because
I stopped drinking that day
on 9th November
on 9th November exactly
yeah
yeah
no no
I didn't
I didn't know
I hadn't heard
I was in hospital
it was a coincidence
dunno
fate
I don't believe in fate
but
it was such a coincidence
that the day I had to
er
stop
the wall came down
I woke up
and I was
doubly
doubly a new person
I started to live without drinking
and in a new society
I'd been drinking
let me think
around ten glasses of beer

and half a bottle of brandy
up to a bottle a day
and it ruined my circulation
I was taken to hospital
and
I dunno
it was like
like
my mum came
and my dad
I was in bed
and
I could see
they'd brought oranges
and I told them:
you shouldn't have
they're pensioners
they could go over
but
I said
it's not Christmas
where did you get the oranges?
You shouldn't have gone to the West
it's not –
No, they said, no
it's not Christmas
but the border's open
yes.
Well
I wondered where I was
whether I was in heaven
but no
I had all my wits about me.
Still
it felt pretty strange.

STRANGER'S HOUSE

by Dea Loher

translated by David Tushingham

Dea Loher was born in Traunstein in Bavaria in 1964 and now lives in Berlin. She studied literature and philosophy in Munich and later playwriting at the Hochschule der Künste, Berlin. She was a participant at the 1993 Royal Court International Summer School for which she won a scholarship from the European Arts Fund. Her plays include *Olga's Raum* (1990), *Tätowierung* (1992), which won the Goethe Award of the Mülheimer Theatertage, and was first presented in English as *Tattoo* in the first German season at the Royal Court Theatre Upstairs in October 1993 with a subsequent production at the New Grove Theatre in London in October 1994, *Leviathan* (1993), *Fremdes Haus* (1995) and *Adam Geist* (1996). In 1995 she received a Schiller Award. Her work has been produced in Hamburg, Berlin, Hannover and Frankfurt and translated into English, Finnish, French, Spanish and Russian.

Characters

YANNE SOKOLOV, *early twenties*
HRISTO MIHAIJLOV, *early sixties*
TERESE MIHAIJLOV, *early fifties*
AGNES, *early twenties, Hristo and Terese's daughter*
JÖRG, *mid twenties, married to Agnes*
NELLY, *mid thirties*

Setting

A run down part of town alongside a canal. There used to be a bridge across the canal, which was demolished, and a remnant of its arch still sticks out over the water.

Special thanks to Gjorgij Jolevskij, Vlado Cvetanovski, Jordan Plevnes and Underground Republic, and to Sinolocka Trpkova.

Stranger's House was first performed in English as a rehearsed
reading in the *New German Voices* season in the Theatre
Upstairs on 4 October 1995 with the following cast:

Nelly	Joanna Bacon
Agnes	Jane Hazelgrove
Jörg	Nicolas Tennant
Terese	June Watson
Hristo	Bernard Kay
Yanne	Gregory Donaldson

Director   John Burgess
Translator   Michael and Michael

The British premiere was staged at the Royal Court Theatre
Upstairs as part of the New European Writers' Season; first
performance on 2 December 1997 with the following cast:

Nelly	Caroline O'Neill
Agnes	Georgina Sowerby
Jörg	Paul Bettany
Terese	Gillian Hanna
Hristo	Christopher Ettridge
Yanne	Matthew Rhys

Director   Mary Peate
Translator   David Tushingham
Designer   Simon Vincenzi
Lighting   Chahine Yavroyan
Sound   Fergus O'Hare

Prologue

Blinded

High, mighty and seemingly impregnable, Czar Samuel's fortress towered over Ohrid when, hungry to extend his rule further, he dispatched an army to Byzantium against Emperor Basil. However, Basil's army destroyed Samuel's between the mountains of Bjelasnica and Ograzden and took the survivors prisoner. Basil had Samuel's soldiers, fifteen thousand of them, blinded in both eyes. The stench of burnt skin and blackened blood hung around for days outside the gates of Byzantium. He spared just one hundred and fifty – these hundred and fifty were only blinded in one eye. And that is how Basil sent them back to Samuel: every hundred blind soldiers led by one with one eye. And when Samuel looked out from his fortress above Ohrid, high, mighty and seemingly impregnable, and saw that procession of wretches, his heart failed.

1. Outside Nelly's Bar

YANNE. I'm looking –

NELLY. Here?

YANNE. I'm looking for –

NELLY. Nobody comes looking for anything here.

Not round this way.

YANNE. I'm looking for Hristo Mihaijlov.

NELLY. Never heard of him.

Silence.

And no one's got anything left worth taking.

This is a godforsaken place.

Round here it's so sad, dogs in the street cry if you so much as look at them.

YANNE. Hristo Mihaijlov.

He's got a shop. Cigarettes and things.

Pause.

NELLY. The Polish tobacconist.

A few doors along. Just follow the canal.

Pause.

Are you from Poland too?

YANNE. Macedonia.

NELLY. Never heard of it.

YANNE. A few doors along in which direction?

NELLY. Macedonia.

Sounds like a godforsaken place.

But all the rarest, most beautiful plants bloom in the most godforsaken places. So I'm told.

Pause.

That way.

YANNE *exits.*

NELLY. What's he come to this godforsaken place for?

Whatever for?

2. Outside the Tobacconist's

YANNE. Are you Hristo Mihaijlov?

HRISTO. What does it look like.

YANNE. So you're him.

HRISTO. It's not a crime.

Is it?

Pause.

YANNE. I, I've come from Ohrid. From home.

Yanne Sokolov, Dimeter's son.

Silence.

HRISTO. Dimeter.

Dimeter Sokolov.

YANNE. That's him.

Your friend Dimeter.

HRISTO (*smokes, coughs*). Unlikely.

Silence.

Enter TERESE.

HRISTO. Now what do you want?

TERESE. I saw a stranger come in and not go out again.
What's he looking for?

YANNE. I'm from Ohrid. Dimeter's son.

My father said that you would have been my godfather only
the times weren't right.

HRISTO. He says he's Dimeter's son. That's what he says. Let him prove it first. Might be something behind this. Mightn't there. How do I know. What do you want?

YANNE. So Goce became my godfather instead.

TERESE. Goce –

YANNE. Yeah. My uncle. Goce, the one who was in Goli otok. (*Pause. To* TERESE.) Do you know what that is, Goli otok, it's a camp, a gulag, you know what I mean –

HRISTO (*smokes, coughs*). Argh, those aren't stories you should be telling in front of ladies.

TERESE. The first one to come here. After how many years?

YANNE. If you try to remember –

I was this high the last time you visited us –

HRISTO (*smokes, coughs*). I have no recollection.

Pause.

And none of that proves anything.

TERESE. What's your mother's name?

YANNE. My mother's name is Despina, like my mother's mother and my mother's mother's mother and my father's name is Dimeter and his father's name is Yanne like me, and my father's father's father's name was Method, my mother's sister is called Denica and my father's brother is called Goce after the famous revolutionary and he used to be your very best –

HRISTO. Do you want him to recite the whole family tree?

TERESE. You were the one who wanted proof. (*To* YANNE.) How long are you going to stay?

HRISTO. What is there to keep anyone here?

He's passing through. Right.

Silence.

YANNE. Well.

Silence.

I've deserted.

HRISTO. Deserted.

YANNE. There's going to be a war.

HRISTO. Ah, so to be on the safe side you just pissed off. Eh. One of them. One of them. You won't be able to hide here.

YANNE. I thought because you did the same yourself –

HRISTO. What –

Because I what –

I was no deserter, picka ti majcina – (*Coughs.*)

never in my life –

YANNE. Of course –

Yes –

That's exactly it.

Deserting's not the right word.

Everybody always told me you did the right thing. That time. When you left –

And now – they had to close the hotel where I was training. Empty rooms. Since the old state collapsed. And its republics. – There's going to be a war. In the next door republic they're conscripting men into the army. And they want us as their allies. – What was I supposed to do? – And then I thought of you. And the ones who always said: do a Hristo. Go.

Silence.

HRISTO. Yeah. And everyone here's been waiting for you. What do you plan to do? What have you learnt? In that hotel of yours.

YANNE. Hotel management.

HRISTO. Ho-tel-man-age-ment –

Is that a polite way of saying cook.

Then you can sell specialities, burek, out of a basket, on street corners. But cheap mind, so people will buy them. And at night, so you don't get caught.

TERESE. Do you know anything about cars?

YANNE. Cars.

TERESE. Well. (*To* HRISTO.) He could help Jörg in the garage.

HRISTO. Just the thing he's been looking for: foreign help.

TERESE. Or he can keep you company in the shop. –

Anyway, Agnes's room is standing empty.

Pause.

HRISTO. Mind you don't regret it. –

I'm company enough for me.

3. In the Garage Yard

AGNES. Just picture it, an entire hotel.

By a lake.

On a hill by a lake. In Ohrid.

And it will belong to him. When he goes back with money.

Just him. He says.

JÖRG. And his wife.

Silence.

AGNES. Some people can go a long way.

Silence.

JÖRG. He can do a lot of talking and as long as the war's still on he'll never have to prove any of it.

AGNES. And from the terrace, he says, if you could fly straight up from the hotel terrace, really high, as high as a falcon, then you can see the sea beyond the Albanian mountains –

Silence.

JÖRG. Business is going to pick up too. Here.

Silence.

AGNES. If I could find a job again.

JÖRG. You've no chance. No one's going to take you on with that leg.

Silence.

AGNES. Sometimes I think we ought to be living an entirely different way.

JÖRG. Really.

AGNES. Yes.

Think it all through again from scratch. Another way.

JÖRG. What do you mean?

Silence.

AGNES. I don't know exactly.

Independent.

To be independent.

JÖRG. You've got me for that.

4. In the Garage Yard

JÖRG. Did the old man send you?

YANNE. Terese did.

I told her I'm not an expert.

JÖRG. Yeah. I heard.

You're destined for better things.

YANNE. I want to open a hotel.

When I go back.

In Ohrid.

Pause.

JÖRG. You can sort the screws out.

YANNE. How much an hour?

JÖRG. As many as you can manage.

Jesus, any fool can do that.

YANNE. No, how much are you going to pay me per hour?

JÖRG. If I could afford to employ help, I wouldn't have had to wait for you. Would I?

YANNE. If I could afford to work for nothing I wouldn't be here. Would I?

Pause.

JÖRG. I can't help you.

There are too many of your kind.

Pause.

It was damned generous. Of Terese. Letting you have the room. Generous I reckon. You ought to make an effort. I reckon. In return.

YANNE. I don't need anybody telling me that. What I owe. I already know without your help.

JÖRG. Something to acknowledge. That you appreciate it. And you realise. What it costs her. Your being the exclusive occupant now. Of that room. You might think of something.

YANNE. Supposing I did take a job for no money. That would be doing you a favour. But I don't owe you anything.

JÖRG. Listen. I don't know where she goes now. Now that the room's no longer free. But wherever she does it. It's none of your business. You got me. There's no need for you to go talking about it. No need for you to go running around, spreading the word. Blabbing it out to everyone all over the place.

Pause.

That's the least. You owe us.

Pause.

Seeing as you're part of the family. Kind of.

YANNE. If I don't know anything. I can hardly give it away. Unless I do it without meaning to.

Pause.

JÖRG. What would you do if your wife was being unfaithful? What do I mean unfaithful? Selling herself. To allcomers.

YANNE. If a woman did marry me. She wouldn't do it to be unfaithful.

JÖRG. A disgrace, a damned –

Yes.

That's what it is.

A disgrace.

Silence.

I'm not saying this because I'm a big moralist. But because she's not alone. If she was on her own she could do whatever she liked. But like this. She doesn't just shame herself, she brings it on the whole family. A shame so deep and so strong, you just can't keep your head up when you walk down the street any more.

Silence.

YANNE. Is this the same room we're talking about? And the same woman?

JÖRG. I don't think it's the money she's doing it for. Well. Since she's been laid off they need every Mark. But. She'd already started before. So.

Pause.

I reckon she's sick.

YANNE. You're making all this up. Why?

JÖRG. I thought you'd known for ages.

YANNE. I don't believe you. Why would she do that to a man like Hristo.

JÖRG. That's what I'm saying. She's sick.

YANNE. If Hristo finds out.

JÖRG. He just stares at the till when the guys come into the shop for cigarettes. On their way home.

YANNE. How come everyone knows and no one does anything?

JÖRG. What I'm most afraid of is this.

If the daughter starts taking after her mother.

Just as long as it doesn't get passed on.

When they hit the change of life. That's when you've really got to watch out. Be prepared. I tell you. If it gets that far with Agnes. I won't know myself any more.

5. On the Bridge

YANNE. Terese and you, you'll be having your silver wedding soon. Won't you.

HRISTO. Mhm.

Look over there.

That's where the rich people live. Trees along the bank.

YANNE. Yes. I can see them from my room. It's a nice room.

Pause.

I remembered her being different somehow, Terese, from that time you visited.

Pause.

But I was still a child.

Silence.

HRISTO (*coughs*). Argh, there are times I've imagined what it would be like sitting here with your mother.

YANNE. With my mother –

HRISTO (*coughs*). You know – I used to – picka ti majcina, I used to really fancy your mother. By Saint Clement, picka ti majcina, I was this close to killing myself because of her –

YANNE. What –

You and my mother –

HRISTO (*smokes*). Well it didn't happen. Your father was quicker than me. Randy little bugger. It was a secret. Your uncle and I, we used to meet secretly with girls in your grandfather's barn, you know what I mean. And we wouldn't let your father in – he was too little. I don't know

how many times he must have been out there with his big
ears burning, glued to the barn door. Miserable little runt.
Well he managed to pick up enough from what he heard.
Argh. I was a fool. I went with all the girls in that barn. All
of them. But just for practice. So I could get really good at
it, you know what I mean. I was waiting for your mother to
be that little bit older. No longer under age. And what
happens. He goes and steals her away from me. Little prick
fucking orthodox cunt bastard — (*Coughs.*)

Silence.

Oh God Oh God. Sveti Kliment forgive me. What am I
saying. I shouldn't talk like that, I know. But it's the passion
inside that's talking. Look at the way my hands are shaking,
even now, all I have to do is think about her.

Silence.

He's treating her alright, isn't he? She's alright with your
father.

YANNE. My mother wasn't the reason you went away though.

HRISTO. 'Course not. You don't go running away because of
some woman. For God's sake.

YANNE. But if you'd been close to killing yourself because of
her.

HRISTO (*smokes, coughs*). Argh, it's a figure of speech. No
sensible man's ever going to do himself in because of a
woman. Nothing against your mother. But – a man's hopes
can always be raised, revived by another woman. That's
what you think anyway. Isn't it. As soon as one leaves, the
next'll come along wiggling her bottom all smiles. – If I'd
wanted to kill myself I wouldn't have emigrated. Nah.

YANNE. Mother never mentioned you.

HRISTO. Right. There we are.

YANNE. My father did though. He says if you hadn't gone,
the same would have happened to you that happened to
Uncle Goce.

HRISTO. Could be. Could be.

YANNE. My father says if Goce had only half your brains he'd have followed your advice and gone off with you. Only he was an idealist, stubborn –

HRISTO. Argh, everyone was an idealist in those days. We had to be to join the partisans. Still anyone could see there was going to be trouble sooner or later. Soon as a man like Tito sets up a secret police. In the beginning we stuck together, we all did, everyone who called themselves Communists – and we were – each man as good as the next, but we were wary because anyone might open his mouth later with some sort of criticism or attack. And rightly so. There were enough attacks. And you'd be branded as a traitor straight away.

YANNE. And that's who they built Goli otok for. The camp on the island.

Silence.

So you and Goce, you went and said too much. – But you had a right to. Hell, you were with the partisans.

HRISTO. Picka ti majcina, I don't want to hear any more about it.

YANNE. Mother never talks about you. That's true. But she's got a picture of you on her dressing table. Before you got caught –

I want to know what that's like –

What they do to you –

when you can't speak any more because your tongue, your lips are so swollen and infected –

and what it was like when they let you go, and you tried to persuade Goce to escape, but he refused; and how he was arrested –

HRISTO. Yanne if you say just one more word, I swear by Saint Method, I'll throw you off this bridge so hard there'll be bones flying in all directions – as far as I'm concerned

the past is dead – finished – leave me alone – leave me
alone – and you – think about where you belong, and stop
trying to play the hero.

6. In Yanne's Room

TERESE. Why are you sitting here in the dark?

YANNE. I'm thinking up a letter.

Pause.

I think it all through, then when it's finished in my head, I write it down.

TERESE. To your girlfriend?

Silence.

YANNE. We were getting married.

Silence.

TERESE. You must take her on a long honeymoon, your – Olga.

YANNE. Yes.

TERESE. The only place Hristo ever took me was Ohrid. You were a little boy then. Do you remember?

YANNE. There are photos.

TERESE. When Goce laid eyes on Hristo for the first time in nearly twenty years. Do you remember. How he offered Hristo his hand, and Hristo took it, the way they threw their arms around each other and danced.

YANNE. They danced?

TERESE. That's what it looked like – you don't have the photos with you by any chance?

YANNE. My father keeps them locked up in his desk.

Silence.

TERESE. How is Goce now?

YANNE. What do you expect? He's an old man.

TERESE. And his wife.

YANNE. Elena – she's dead. Goce's alone.

Pause.

He talks about Hristo, a lot.

TERESE. Hristo's got to tell you. The whole story. Everything.
– I thought he was a coward for a long time. And I was
afraid I would start despising him for it. But I've always
stuck by him, I never abandoned him.

Pause.

Perhaps that was wrong.

Pause.

The suspicion, that suspicion in his eyes, perhaps it wasn't
suspicion at all. But fear.

Pause.

He should have trusted me. If only he could have trusted
me. And not just me. – I would never have left him. I never
have left him. All I wanted was to live openly. Not hiding
anything.

Silence.

Forgiveness only counts from the person you've wronged,
doesn't it. No one else. No one else.

Silence.

YANNE. Hristo's not a coward. And your private life is none
of my business, I think.

TERESE. But it is, it is. You ask him, go on, ask him about the
past.

YANNE. Alright.

TERESE. Good. Good. Good.

Silence.

(*Indicating the letter.*) I imagine she misses you a lot?

YANNE. Her letter's meant to give that impression.

TERESE. Read it to me.

YANNE. What?

TERESE. Read it to me.

I want to know what a love letter sounds like.

YANNE. No.

Silence.

I can't do that.

Silence.

It would be like taking all her clothes off in front of you.

TERESE. Yes.

Silence.

A nice thought.

Somehow.

7. In the Garage Yard

a.

AGNES. He's started a dealership. Next to the garage. Used cars.

The first time I saw him I thought, he's got a head for business.

Pause.

Yes. That's what he really wants, to be a car dealer. A proper one.

YANNE. Mercedes BMW Ferrari.

AGNES. That sort of price range.

YANNE. He's got some work to do.

AGNES. So do you.

Pause.

But the economy here's not helping.

b.

JÖRG. Deserting –

But you've got to make peace with your enemies.

Eventually.

YANNE. Do you?

JÖRG. That's not in your book is it.

YANNE. In your book. Are you afraid I'm a Muslim? I don't read the Koran. My passport says: Orthodox.

c.

AGNES. It was an accident.

YANNE. Was it his fault?

AGNES. He's going too fast. And I run straight out into the
road without looking. Next thing I know, I'm waking up in
hospital with my knee swollen the size of a child's head.

YANNE. It's one way of getting to know people.

AGNES. He took care of me.

Very good care.

That's not something I'm used to.

Pause.

Told me about his garage. Like it was this place just waiting
for me.

Silence.

YANNE. Will you ever walk properly again?

AGNES. It's hopeless.

But he's made one promise.

If it stiffens up completely, he'll get them to give me an
artificial knee.

d.

JÖRG. And I've never been able to work out, I still haven't,
what a Macedonian actually is and how they can be any
different from a Serb or an Albanian or a Croat or a
Montenegran.

e.

AGNES. What about your girlfriend – she must be patient?

Silence.

YANNE. Her letters are like news bulletins. Stick to the facts.
– I suspect she doesn't want to alarm me with any
uncontrollable feelings of longing.

AGNES. If I were in her shoes –

I wouldn't want to wait.

8. In Yanne's Room

TERESE (*smells*). Mmh, that's more like it – that's real after-shave.

YANNE. It's only cheap.

TERESE. It's ages since this room had the smell of a man.

YANNE. I'll do my best not to change your room too much, not so much that you won't recognise it, not so much that you won't know your way round any more.

TERESE. I used to come here for a lie down in the afternoons.

YANNE. Ye-es – I heard something like that.

TERESE. And originally we were going to turn it into an office. This room. For Hristo. And I was going to hand in my notice at the factory, all official, and I would do the accounts here and all the paperwork.

Pause.

Like it was our own little company.

Silence.

But things never got that far. The shop doesn't bring enough in.

Pause.

And now we're glad of my dole money.

YANNE. But you're earning on the side.

Silence.

TERESE. So?

Silence.

TERESE. Shall I do it for nothing in your case?

Silence.

(*Laughs.*) How much do you think I can make, eh –

Pause.

(*Laughs.*) A fortune, when you're my age.

Pause.

And you look like me. Well.

Silence.

It's just a couple of gentlemen from the firm who still feel some sort of attachment to me, maybe they feel guilty because I was one of the ones they sacked. They're too old, too cowardly, too lazy, what do I know, to go out on the streets looking, and they're not rich enough to be choosy. So I've got an advantage. And I can provide them with relief, in more ways than one.

YANNE. And why does it have to happen here, so everyone knows?

TERESE. Before you start getting disgusted – you ought to ask Hristo what deception means. What betrayal is. – None of it was my idea.

YANNE (*angered*). Your private life is no concern of mine. And don't worry, I'm not going to be stopping in your room for very much longer and depriving you of your income if that's what you're afraid of. Before I turn into a parasite I'll be off.

TERESE (*very calm*). It's just a business. It keeps me alive. It's got nothing to do with my heart.

9. On the Bridge

HRISTO. I took my time. Through Hungary and Austria. Lived off the black market. Started out doing a bit of smuggling and gradually expanded. Till I got stuck with cigarettes. I did some good deals back then. Macedonian tobacco, picka ti majcina, some folk still lick their lips at the mention of it today.

YANNE. So you were in the same position as me. Trying to hold on to your life and make something out of it.

HRISTO. Hey – don't you compare yourself with me. Don't compare yourself with me. I ran away because the people I was fighting with side by side for a free country, because they betrayed me the moment they got their hands on a little power. And they claimed that I'd let down our common cause, me. They had no ears for criticism, know what I mean. – (*Smokes.*) I had a good reason to get out. But you. What do you want? You and your war that's only an excuse. What kind of ideas have you got in your head?

YANNE. I want us to have a better life too.

HRISTO. Us, who's us?

YANNE. My – our family. Friends. Everyone.

HRISTO. Did you just read that in the Bible or something? A humanitarian. My arse. What are you really? What are your beliefs? Are you a communist? A socialist? A democrat? A fucking liberal?

YANNE. I don't know I –

I –

I'm –

I believe –

I'm a Macedonian –

HRISTO. Macedonian, Macedonian –

What does that mean? Is that some kind of philosophy?
What are you trying to say? You're a Nationalist?

YANNE. No.

HRISTO (*smokes, coughs*). So what are you doing here?

The truth is it's your own idleness which has dragged you
here and the corruption at home is a welcome excuse.

YANNE. I don't want any favours.

HRISTO. Yeah. You want to work. What for? What for?

Prosperity.

Picka ti majcina –

There've been elections, haven't there, the first free
elections for an independent republic. And you want to be
here.

YANNE. Because no one can tell whether it'll survive the war.

HRISTO. In those days I would have been glad to be in a
country that knows what a democratic election looks like.

YANNE (*groans*). Hristo – it might look like it. But how many
of the people who are getting elected now, shared out
between different lists and all shouting Democracy,
Democracy at the tops of their voices, are exactly the same
ones as before.

HRISTO. And can you say that out loud at home, can you?
Can you pass on your opinion out loud in public to anyone
who's willing to listen?

YANNE. Ye-es.

HRISTO. Then go back and do it.

10. In Yanne's Room

YANNE. What have you got there?

AGNES. Nothing.

YANNE. There's a bit too much cloth there for nothing.

He takes the suit from her and inspects it.

The elbows are worn through. The collar's as shiny as a rat's coat. – A pin-stripe. – I thought that was out of fashion. This button's been sewn back on again. Blue thread instead of black, it doesn't look right. There again. Depends what it's for – where are you taking it?

AGNES. It's Jörg's. I was taking it to the cleaners.

YANNE. You've got money for that.

Silence.

YANNE. It was that poor Macedonian guy you were taking it to. As charity. Your heart full of good deeds. You thought he's bound to be pleased. Poor devil. Coming from a country where they still wear cloths tied round their feet instead of shoes. So he'll be grateful for every rag on his back. Was that what you were thinking?

AGNES. No, that's not what I was thinking –

I thought –

The suit – Jörg got caught out in the rain in it. – It's got mud splashes from the bottoms up to the knees and an oil stain on the sleeve. – And on top of that it's his favourite pub suit, drenched in that atmosphere of chips and beer. – It stinks, it stinks, here, smell it – and that's why I was taking it to the cleaners.

YANNE. You forgot piss.

AGNES. What –

YANNE. You forgot the smell of piss. Pub air and the gents, they always go together.

AGNES. Ye-es – look at this – it's spit.

YANNE. And sick.

AGNES. And sweat –

Pause.

YANNE. Did he send it? The suit.

Silence.

I want to know what's behind this. Whether he's trying to prove something or not.

Silence.

AGNES. He is trying to prove something, but it's not his worst suit.

Silence.

And what am I to do with it now?

YANNE. It's not his worst one.

AGNES. No.

YANNE. Then leave it here.

11. In Nelly's Bar

NELLY. I named the drink after you, when people ask I tell them it's a Polish speciality.

YANNE. I'm not from Poland.

NELLY. Who cares.

YANNE. What do I owe you?

NELLY. It's on the house.

The customers like talking to you.

YANNE. No one's said more than ten words to me.

NELLY. Except me, I talk to you.

And I look at you.

Silence.

YANNE. Maybe I like it.

Maybe I don't like it.

NELLY. 'Course you like it.

YANNE. My long-term intentions aren't in this area.

NELLY. So there's all the more reason to grab your chance.

Silence.

I took the bar because it's on the canal. How many years now have I been going outside to gaze across the water. Where beautiful men go walking along the promenade. Secretly hoping that one of these days one of them might find his way here.

YANNE. I've already promised as much as I can.

NELLY. I don't trust promises.

YANNE. There's someone waiting for me. At home.

NELLY. Never mind that, Polack.

YANNE. This is a very temporary stay.

NELLY. Certain needs never go away.

Pause.

YANNE. Come on then.

12. By the canal

JÖRG. Hoping to meet someone.

YANNE. I've taken up your habit of an evening walk by the canal.

Who are you waiting for?

JÖRG. Look up on the bridge. Right up there, where that iron girder's sticking out of the concrete and it's made a little hollow, there's a falcon hiding there.

YANNE. No chance. You're joking.

JÖRG. I've been watching it.

YANNE. You're wrong. It's probably a buzzard. A sparrowhawk maybe. Never a falcon.

JÖRG. 'Course it is. The way it floats on the wind, the spread of its wings, the shape of its beak and its call – it's a falcon alright.

YANNE. What sort of prey is a falcon going to find in the city?

JÖRG. Squirrels. There are loads of rabbits in that park over there. Rats where it can get them.

YANNE. No chance.

JÖRG. Are you saying I'm a liar?

YANNE. Are you saying I'm thick?

JÖRG. Anyhow it won't survive. I've been watching. I'll give it an outside chance.

YANNE. If it's a falcon, it'll survive. Because it won't know what fear is.

Silence.

JÖRG. It's a good fit, that suit of mine.

YANNE. Apparently it's not your worst.

JÖRG. No. It wasn't cheap.

But I'm sure you'll be able to afford better once you're back home and you've opened up that hotel of yours.

YANNE. Maybe I like it so much here I'll never go back.

JÖRG. There isn't room for everyone. People who don't succeed and have ambitions.

YANNE. But you've got plenty to spare. Suits, for example, when you're feeling particularly generous.

JÖRG. Why don't you just go. Keep the damned suit and fuck off. What can you do here? Sit round waiting. And go causing trouble where there wasn't any before.

YANNE. So you'd go and fight in the war, if you were me.

JÖRG. But running off like that is demeaning.

Pause.

YANNE. Have you ever seen anyone die?

JÖRG. No, I haven't.

YANNE. Or a dead body, have you ever seen a dead body?

JÖRG. No.

YANNE. But you'd be ready to kill someone?

JÖRG. Yes I would. I would. If they were threatening me, me or my wife, my wife, then I'd kill them.

Pause.

What about you, have you seen a dead body?

YANNE. Yes.

JÖRG. And have you ever seen anyone die?

YANNE. Yes, I have.

JÖRG. Probably your grannie, eh.

YANNE. So you're not like me, you wouldn't run away.

JÖRG. I'd defend my business. Myself. My family's livelihood.

YANNE. So if one day, tomorrow, possibly today, let's say right now, I was waiting for you as it was getting dark, in a doorway, round a corner, or here behind this pillar, in a shadow, and suddenly I was to step out into the light when I heard your footsteps getting really close – and I'd got a knife in my hand –

He pulls a knife out of his jacket pocket and lets it spring open.

JÖRG. Then you wouldn't scare me.

YANNE. I wouldn't? Because I've got to be grateful to you, is that it, that's what you reckon, what you're counting on, on the gratitude I must feel for your shitty suit the one you sent your wife with, because you're too shy to look me in the eye – is that it –

JÖRG. I – I'm not going to let myself be provoked –

YANNE. What kind of shitty deal is this you're offering me, sending me your shitty suit and showing me your hungry falcon and acting like you're doing me some big favour. When what you actually want to do is deceive me. You want me to take these gifts of yours and go all soft and keep out of your life. Is that it? But you wouldn't share your business with me, and you wouldn't let your wife go with me –

JÖRG. You've got no right – no right – that's not a fair fight – I've got no weapon –

YANNE. It's not any kind of fight. That's not the way I do things. Take off your jacket.

JÖRG. I've not got my wallet with me.

YANNE. Take your jacket off.

JÖRG *does it.*

JÖRG. You've got no right to my life.

YANNE. Your shitty life. Take your shirt off. And those
trousers.

JÖRG. I'm telling you, I've got no money on me.

YANNE. Money money.

JÖRG. It's a hard life. I work hard for my life.

YANNE. Remember, I've watched people die. And if I decide
to cut your throat for you now, then your shitty life is going
to be over. That hard shitty life will be gone. How happy
you'll be. – Take your shirt off. And your trousers.

JÖRG *does it.*

YANNE. Climb up on the railing. –

What are you staring at me for?

JÖRG *does it.*

JÖRG. I – I was trying to help you.

YANNE. Get up on that railing.

JÖRG *does it.*

YANNE. Now jump.

JÖRG. The water's less than ten degrees.

YANNE. Jump.

JÖRG *jumps.*

YANNE *takes his clothes off and puts* JÖRG*'s new suit on.*

YANNE. You see I like wearing your suits. When they're new.

And watch out for that falcon. It might think you're a canal
rat.

Exit.

13. In the Garage Yard

TERESE. Yanne's got a job.

Pause.

AGNES. I heard. Cleaning in a bar.

TERESE. You know something better.

JÖRG. She's worried about him.

TERESE. You worry about your own husband, not strangers.

AGNES. And just who is this advice coming from?

JÖRG. Terese has got eyes.

Enter HRISTO.

HRISTO. Yanne's got a job.

JÖRG. Cleaning in a bar. Ten Marks an hour.

HRISTO. So. He might earn more than you.

JÖRG. Yeah. He's already worth more than me. Isn't he.

HRISTO. Argh. If you will go jumping into the canal like a rat. I mean who was after you? The police looking for car ringers.

AGNES. Leave him alone. – And keep your nose out of his business.

HRISTO (*smokes*). Well you're the right one to be speaking up. Acting all loyal now. Argh. But as soon as he's got his back turned – picka ti majcina . . . we should keep our noses out of your business. Argh. If that's what you're trying to say. You'll soon be competing with your mother.

JÖRG. Hey, Agnes believes in true love. She'd never do it for money.

Sudden, deep silence. Glances towards TERESE.

TERESE (*slowly*). So this is how you talk about me. When I'm not listening. And smile to my face when I'm looking at you.

Silence.

(*Softly.*) What have I done? What have I done?

Silence.

Enter YANNE.

YANNE. I've found a job.

Silence.

Hey. What's the matter? I've got a job. – Cleaning. In a bar. Ten Marks an hour.

JÖRG. So this is the big break is it?

HRISTO (*coughs*). They're really ripping you off. At ten Marks an hour they're ripping you right off.

YANNE. How come? Five hours three times a week makes fifty, hundred and fifty, times four – six hundred Marks a month, cash in hand, at home it takes me three months to earn that much. And this is just the beginning.

HRISTO. As long as there's no catch.

YANNE. Looks like I can move out soon. Won't be scrounging off you any longer. – And the room'll be free again.

Silence.

TERESE. Stay.

Silence.

Stay here. Stay here.

HRISTO (*coughs*). You're not scrounging off us.

JÖRG. You can afford it.

AGNES. There's no reason to go.

YANNE. Yes there is.

Silence.

But there are a couple of things to clear up first. – Like I've not told you the truth about Goce.

TERESE. Everything'll be alright. Everything'll be alright.

HRISTO. Not now surely.

TERESE. Speak. Speak.

YANNE. It's true that Goce's been living on his own since Elena died. But I didn't tell you how she died.

HRISTO. We don't want to know, we don't want to know.

TERESE. You speak for yourself, Hristo. Keep talking.

YANNE. Goce and Elena were married for twenty-seven years. Quite an achievement. Wasn't it. Out of those twenty-seven years Goce spent fourteen in Goli otok. While Elena waited for him. – Because she saw that as her duty.

HRISTO. She loved him – you idiot. If you've any idea what that word means.

YANNE. When Goce came back from the camp, he was deaf in one ear, crippled down one side and – er he'd become er depressed.

Silence.

Elena never complained. They seemed to belong together without question.

AGNES. What did he do to her?

YANNE. All those years Elena had been having an affair with another man. I don't know whether she was ever really unfaithful to Goce. I mean –

HRISTO (*coughs*). Right. So it was a beautiful unbodily love. As clean as the Virgin Mary's sheets.

YANNE. It's important that Goce didn't suspect anything. And he – he was content with his life. With Elena. D'you understand. Agnes. He was as – as –

HRISTO. Content –

YANNE. Happy as anyone in his situation could be.

Silence.

During all that time Elena must have considered leaving him. But she never went through with it. She thought she owed him something.

Pause.

And then, after twenty-seven years, this man, her lover, convinced her to go away with him. So Elena tidies up the flat. One last time. Makes the beds once more. Empties her wardrobe. And packs her suitcase. She dresses for the journey. Comfortable shoes, a light dress and a warm jacket. Puts on her hat and pins it in place. Picks up her gloves in one hand and her handbag in the other. Checks one last time that she's got all her things. Papers money purse. Closes the bag again. And sits down on the bed. Ready to go.

Silence.

AGNES. And.

YANNE. When the man came to pick her up she was dead. She was sitting on the bed. Her head resting against the wall. And she was dead.

Silence.

JÖRG. Poor Goce.

AGNES. What a beautiful death.

JÖRG. What –

AGNES. I think it's a beautiful death.

HRISTO. She's not got that idea from me. I didn't bring her up to such perversion.

TERESE. It's not perverse. It's – logical.

YANNE. Yes. That's right.

TERESE. You know what I'm talking about, Hristo.

HRISTO. I know alright. A woman who'd sooner die than betray her husband.

TERESE. How horribly you can twist the truth. Did you know, did you know that about Goce. Are you going to lie about this too if it suits you?

HRISTO. For the umpteenth time stop getting at me. What crime have I ever done you? (*To* YANNE.) Yes, it's about time you were gone. I don't give a fuck where. I just don't want to see your face again.

Exits. TERESE *goes after him.*

JÖRG. Don't let yourself be talked into anything by him, Agnes.

YANNE. I'm not forcing anyone to do anything.

JÖRG. You heard. You're not wanted here any more.

YANNE. I'm not asking you.

Exits.

AGNES. Where are you going?

YANNE. To breathe.

AGNES *hesitates, goes after him, looks round at* JÖRG, *exits.*

14. Outside the Tobacconist's

HRISTO. You're not starting that again.

TERESE. Well we can't go on like this. You should have told him the truth back then, in Ohrid. Instead of celebrating a reunion.

HRISTO. What good would that have done?

TERESE. You wouldn't have spent your whole life living a damned lie. And letting them think you'd been trying to save Goce when you really betrayed him. It's despicable. Letting them think you're a hero. Letting them worship you, and tell their children stories about how clever and brave Hristo was with Goce grinning beside you like an idiot. You are such a cowardly bastard.

HRISTO (*smokes, coughs*). They're the ones who've made up the stories and keep embroidering them, it wasn't any of my doing. The last thing I wanted was to see them again, I didn't want to have to speak to them again as long as I lived.

TERESE. Didn't want to have to look them in the eye.

HRISTO. No, I didn't want to have to look them in the eye. – Forget the whole thing it's over. – I can't give him back the years he spent in the camp. Can I.

TERESE. Too right you can't.

HRISTO. I can't give him his hearing back, can I. I can't make him able to move his right arm again or his leg. Can I. Can I do that? – I'm not going to be able to take his depression away.

TERESE. No.

HRISTO. So what would be the good of telling him the truth? The truth. Am I now supposed to take away his belief too, that I'm his friend, possibly the only one he really has faith in, who he doesn't doubt.

TERESE. How on earth can you be so presumptuous. What sort of sick hypocrite are you. What justification can you possibly have –

HRISTO. Terese, Goce has spent his life believing that he went to the camp for his convictions, that he stood up for his – ideals, and that he didn't let himself be manipulated or bribed. That's probably the only way he survived the camp at all, because he thought he was standing up for the right thing, the just thing. Do you understand what I'm saying? Am I supposed to take away this belief he has in himself? Am I supposed to say to him, well mate, you really didn't have much choice, they would have arrested you anyway because – I had betrayed you –

Silence.

TERESE. Yes. That's what you should have done. – You still can do it.

HRISTO (*smokes, coughs*). Stop it stop it. – And I don't need you telling me what to do. Of all people.

TERESE. How you despise me.

Silence.

HRISTO. Yanne didn't tell Elena's story for my benefit.

TERESE. But you're responsible. She only stayed with him out of pity.

HRISTO. You confront me with my conscience but you're the one, you're the one who's brought disgrace into this house, here into my own house, not me. – And do you know, have you seen the way I walk down the street here, I keep my eyes down and stick to the edge of the pavement and what it is that makes me speak only words of one syllable and walk around bent double isn't what I did in the past, it's what my wife makes no secret of the fact she's continuing to do now.

Silence.

TERESE. We should never have gone to Ohrid. – Then I would never have known. And we'd still get on with each other, like we did in the beginning.

HRISTO (*smokes*). It was your idea. I was in no hurry to make the journey.

TERESE. You wouldn't speak to me again afterwards. Hardly even looked at me. – What could I have hoped for?

Silence.

HRISTO. It was because I had to. I was forced to, my life was at stake. – You can't say that. Letting anybody pay you for some dirty satisfaction, that's something you decided to do. – And all the time I've been standing alone in my shop, I've waited in vain for an answer. – Whether there's any sense of shame left inside you.

Silence.

Can you hear me. I want to know whether you've still got a sense of shame. Or have they fucked it out of you, a little bit each, till there was none left, have they, answer –

TERESE. Yes they have.

Pause.

But you were the one who started it.

HRISTO. Then I'm going to finish it too. Right to the end. From now on you can set up shop in the street, do you understand? I don't want to see our daughter getting any ideas from you.

TERESE. You want to put me out on the streets.

HRISTO. You don't see how ashamed you make her. – And how much unhappiness she has to put up with from being married to the bloke you talked her into.

TERESE. What do you imagine –

HRISTO. Don't you notice how she avoids you, the way she bends over when she has to talk to her mother, she despises

you, she despises you for what you do in your room, and
for persuading her to take that Jörg. You can't treat a
marriage like a business deal.

TERESE. You're trying to say – I made my daughter a whore –

HRISTO. I'm not trying, I'm doing it.

TERESE. I don't know you any more. I don't know you any
more. What are you doing –

HRISTO. And I don't know you any more either.

Pause.

Who are you –

15. By the Canal

YANNE. Now

    now

    and now

AGNES. What

YANNE. j-o-y

    and now

    another one

AGNES. What

YANNE. A moment of j-o-y –

AGNES. Fucking always makes me think of death.

YANNE. Even now.

AGNES. It goes away again afterwards.

YANNE. You need to think of death to be able to feel the j-o-y.

AGNES. That's sad.

YANNE. Life ought to be made up of a whole series of
    moments like this, each one experienced to the full – even if
    all they bring is pain – just don't waste a minute, a second –

AGNES. It's a nightmare.

YANNE. Or even better – feel j-o-y – and keep feeling it and
    feeling it – then die.

    Silence.

    Die –

    Silence.

YANNE. Do you think I'm a coward too?

AGNES. No.

YANNE. Do you think I'm a coward too?

AGNES. No.

YANNE. I asked whether you think I'm a coward.

AGNES. Fucking makes me sad and you deaf.

YANNE. I don't believe you. Everyone thinks I'm a coward.

Silence.

Yeah. Maybe. I'll go back.

They talk about duty, sticking together, loving your country.
They talk about honour. They talk about freedom. – But
they never mention the most important thing. –

Perhaps I just need to make the effort. – And it would be no
different from any other job. – Something that needs to be
done – killing.

Silence.

And it's so easy to do once you've made your mind up. –
How much easier it is than stabbing with a knife, pulling
the trigger of a gun towards you, no more than a squeeze of
your finger – and the bullet is on its way.

Silence.

And – if it's that simple – if it's simple and can be done
over and over again – with no difficulty no pain – it might
be – beautiful.

Maybe it doesn't even hurt to be killed. – We have no idea
what it's like, dying –

Yanneyanne or The Drowned Child

YANNE. . . . I keep seeing him here in front of me,
    unexpectedly, in the street, on a bus. In my nights. He was
    my best friend. He was called Yanne like me and he was a
    year older. People got so used to regarding us as inseparable
    every time they saw us they'd shout: Look, here comes
    Yanneyanne. In the Autumn when I was five Yanne picked

me up one morning to go and collect apples. There was an old tree we knew, we couldn't reach the branches but we'd be able to pick up all the apples lying on the ground. It was a cold morning, misty. We'd each taken a toy bucket with us and they were soon full. The apples had wet leaves and earth sticking to them. I can't remember whose idea it was to wash them in the nearby canal. We knew a place where some steps led straight down into the water. The sluice gates were all wide open because there'd been several days of heavy rain before and the water in the canal was very high, it was dark and it had clay and torn-off leaves, bits of bark and small plants all whirling round in there. Yanne went down the steps first. It was only a single movement, dipping his bucket into the current, the water was so quick. I was amazed to see him suddenly get swept away, on his back, clinging on to the bucket which bobbled up and down beside him like a spare head, empty, and the apples floating heavy in the water. And there was no noise. Yanne didn't make a sound, he didn't scream, he didn't shout for me, he just looked at me, he was amazed too. He opened his mouth, the water sped him away and we'd been separated, there was a short gurgling sound, a spinning in the water, then nothing.

Silence.

I didn't understand what had happened. I stood there, holding my bucket with the apples in it in both hands, staring at the steps, the water. Then I ran. And began to scream. I screamed and cried so loud every window in my path flew open and heads stuck out. I ran to the nearest building, stopped right in the middle of the yard and screamed and cried still keeping tight hold of my bucket. No one could get any sense out of me. They wanted to take me to my mother but I wouldn't let them touch me and ran off again into the next building. And I stood there with my bucket screaming. And when they asked me I screamed Yanne's swimming in the canal. Over and over, just that one sentence. Yanne's swimming in the canal. Then they understood what I didn't understand. And they rushed off with ropes and poles.

Silence.

It took a long time for me to take it in. There would be no Yanneyanne any more. Only Yanne was left. Now I had to play by myself most of the time, other children were kept away from me. A railing was put up along the canal bank. I started to wonder what I'd done. Had I pushed him, had my bucket given him a shove. But I hadn't done anything. I'd just wondered what's Yanne doing in the water. And then I imagined what it would be like to drown and to be pulled out of the sluicegates on a hook, like an enormous dead fish.

Yanne's mother's face was pale from that day on. I'd meet her in the street sometimes. And she'd say hello in a very quiet voice, gently. Different from the other grown-ups, who'd often look straight past me. She'd say: Good morning – Yanne. Good morning – Yanne. With that little pause between those words. Her voice haunted me. Because I knew what she must be thinking. I knew what they all thought. I was thinking the same thing. – Yanneyanne was dead. But Yanne's still alive.

Silence.

AGNES. Can you imagine staying here?

For a long time. For ever.

YANNE. Can you imagine leaving here?

For a long time. For ever. Going to my country.

AGNES. Ohrid –

YANNE. I've sent Olga three letters.

And no reply.

AGNES. Staying would be easier.

Silence.

YANNE. What's the most important thing in your life? The most important thing of all, so important, that you'd die if you couldn't do it and your life would have been meaningless –

AGNES. I don't know.

YANNE. You don't know.

AGNES. It's all the same in my life.

YANNE. What sort of questions are you asking me then?

AGNES. I don't know. There's nothing in my life that I absolutely have to do.

Some things are important, others are less important, that much is true. But nothing to put above all else.

YANNE. But you must have desires.

AGNES. No –

Yes.

I'm happy.

YANNE. Don't you ever wish you could walk properly again?

AGNES. Of course.

YANNE. But you're happy.

AGNES. I've come to terms with it. – The leg – losing my job – I've damned well come to terms with it. –

Yes – I'm being cheated out of life – but what can I do about it –

YANNE. But if it's like that why don't you have the operation now? Or does Jörg have to wait so he can get value for money?

AGNES. Why do you want me to be unhappy? Am I supposed to feel bad because I can say that I'm happy?

YANNE. If you're happy why do you want me to stay, just to help you pass the time? –

All I want is to hear once, tell me, why you married this guy, come on tell me, I want to hear it out loud, so I can believe it. And so I can stifle my doubts with your own words.

Silence.

AGNES. You tried to kill him. –

You tried to kill Jörg.

YANNE *shakes his head slowly.*

AGNES. Your doubts.

About what.

Silence.

That there's something that lasts.

Silence.

It's not my fault she hasn't written to you for ages. Your
Olga.

YANNE. I'm not thinking about her. Now.

Silence.

AGNES. I think I did it because –

I thought –

it would turn our family into something better. My mother's
been waiting all her life. Waiting. For someone to rescue
her –

I admire her. I despise her. I love her.

And I'm not like her. I'm not going to hold all my hopes
and feelings out in front of me, offering them to any and
everyone, each time expecting him to want to take them
from my hands and hold them reverently in his, like some
priceless delicate object that has to be treated very carefully
all the time.

That's why I married Jörg. Because I didn't believe in
anything more than an agreement. Because I didn't want to
rely on anything more than a contract.

And I thought that we could make it with the garage. Over
on to the other side of the canal. –

But we won't make it. We're slipping further and further
behind –

YANNE. I understand. –

You got your sums wrong.

Silence.

AGNES. You think Jörg is a hopeless dirty little crook – but he's stuck by me –

YANNE. You admit it. It was a trade-off. It was a deal.

AGNES. Yes. It was a deal.

But that doesn't mean I don't have any feelings for him.

YANNE. Of course not. Gratitude, I expect. He's grateful to you, you're grateful to him, you're both at the mercy of each other's gratitude.

AGNES. I can understand why Olga's not writing to you. She's probably glad to see the back of you. I would be in her shoes and I'd hope you never came back – get yourself an animal you can bully but keep away from human beings because you're not one of them –

Exits.

16. In the Garage Yard

JÖRG. Terese's swimming in the canal. Terese's swimming in the canal.

HRISTO. Stop it.

JÖRG. Dead fish always float belly up. When human beings are dead in the water, they just lie there bloated, in whatever position they died, face up or face down.

YANNE. Shut up, that's no way to talk when someone's died.

JÖRG. You didn't find her, you won't be having bad dreams. But I'm going to be seeing dead bodies every night floating down the canal one after another.

Silence.

AGNES. She always used to smell of lavender. – She often talked about travelling. She liked going for walks by the canal. –

Pause.

But I didn't know her. She was my mother and I didn't know her.

JÖRG. There's no sense in wondering about that any more.

Pause.

We're always told not to speak ill of the dead. As if the dead are better people simply for being dead.

Pause.

She'll have had her reason.

YANNE. Do you know what you are, you slimy little piece of shit.

JÖRG. Fuck off you Balkan bastard, you're not telling me to shut up, a deserter who's run away, they used to shoot people like you, and quite right too.

YANNE. Oh, you're talking about that war you were in, yeah –

AGNES. You're both as pathetic as each other. When I see you I can understand why my mother made men pay because any decent feeling is too good, it would be wasted on the likes of you – I understand her –

Silence.

(*To* HRISTO.) No, I don't understand her, I can't understand her . . . tell me what it was she was carrying round inside her, tell me, what it was you weren't speaking about, so what you did talk about stood out for being so pointless; tell me, give me a reason –

Silence.

HRISTO (*smokes, softly*). Atonement.

Pause.

She'd paid for me.

She'd paid for me the same way Goce had paid for me before, with his life. Two people.

YANNE. Hristo Hristo. Goce wasn't your fault. You both did what was right – and you were just luckier.

HRISTO. Luck –

Luck –

A rotten life.

Look, Yanne, one rotten life –

Coughs.

I know you think it's pitiful and you're right.

There's no shine to it and it can't be shown off with pride –

Coughs.

No. Let me finish.

Because you're wrong if you think this rotten, this faded, worn out life might at least have the saving grace of never abandoning its principles. Of always opting for humanity when asked to choose between it and reason, so the thin cloak life wraps around itself never bore a trace of blood. The two could never be combined. Morality was always at odds with reason, and you had to sell one of them if you wanted to hold onto the other. And I'm telling you if the price I have to pay is as high as the deal I made was damnable, even this threadbare life would seem like a reward.

Coughs heavily.

No, let me finish talking.

Coughs.

Yanne –

Goce paid for me –

Goce paid for me with his life.

YANNE. Picka ti majcina – He knew what was waiting for him in Goli otok. And he still wouldn't go with you. How could you have made him –

Pause.

HRISTO. I betrayed him.

Silence.

It was me who betrayed Goce.

Silence.

And Terese could tell. From when we were together. And the moment we arrived in Ohrid she knew how right she was. – No one there had the slightest suspicion. But she knew. Straight away. As soon as she set eyes on Goce. And from the way I gave him my hand. Yanne, my hands were dripping wet, like I'd been holding them out in the rain. – And I looked Goce in the eye, I did that too. – All of them. I looked them all in the eye. – It should have been enough to make me blind. – I'd never have gone back there. Not ever. Only Terese. For Terese's sake.

Coughs.

Goce was deaf in one ear and crippled down his right side. He held his left hand out to me, like this. -- I – can never make it better, never – nothing – if I could believe – but there's no – I can't – I can't do it –

Silence.

Why don't you say something? Don't you believe me.

YANNE *shakes his head slowly.*

HRISTO. They arrested me. – It's true what your father says, my mouth, my tongue was all swollen up and I couldn't speak, I was spitting pus instead of talking. That's true. But they didn't make me give away Goce's hiding place. They can't make you. You can't do things against your own will. They bought me. My life for his. My escape for his arrest.

Coughs heavily.

I was a coward.

I was afraid.

I was so afraid.

My best friend.

Silence.

It was a deal.

Silence.

YANNE. So it was all lies. You never tried to help him escape.

HRISTO. They released me. We had a secret rendezvous. It was all a game, they already knew where he was hiding. I pleaded with him to escape. But that was a game too. They would have got him instantly. – He didn't want to leave his family alone. – So I left, under surveillance, over the border. Without him. – They waited two days. And then –

That was the deal.

JÖRG. How stupid can your family be never to even suspect anything, and now –

HRISTO. No. – The mere possibility of suspicion would seem like betrayal to them.

Coughs.

And Terese never forgave me for it. She never forgave me for my silence.

(*To* AGNES.) And now you can all despise me too, like she did.

AGNES. – No –

YANNE. Forgiveness –

That you can even think of that –

I'm not sorry for you.

HRISTO. If you went back, Yanne. It'd be only right. Your place isn't here.

YANNE. Never tell me what I have to do again. I don't have to pay for what you owe. Don't ever talk to me about obligations again – You're wrong, they can make you betray people, kill people, but I've not got that far yet, and if I ever do get that far then I would hate myself, do you hear me – yeah, you're not deaf like Goce – I would hate myself for the rest of my life – hate so much that my own hate would kill me – and that's what you've got coming, you hear – hate.

17. In Yanne's Room

AGNES. The doctor says he won't recover.

It's shown up on his lung.

JÖRG. It's all his fault –

If only he'd never come here.

AGNES. I'll stay here as long as Hristo needs me.

Silence.

JÖRG. How long is that going to be?

AGNES. The doctor says tonight or tomorrow.

JÖRG. He's exaggerating.

It's his job.

Pause.

Then I'll stay too.

We can wait together.

AGNES. Don't go and see him just because he's dying.

JÖRG. It was more for your sake.

AGNES. There's no need then.

Silence.

JÖRG. I could rent one of those units. Further up the canal. One of the bigger ones. Could pay for itself. I could put a better workshop in there.

AGNES. Hristo is dying in there.

What are you going on about.

JÖRG. Two funerals so soon after each other.

Someone's got to think about paying for them.

AGNES. Once Hristo doesn't need me any more, we can go our separate ways.

Silence.

JÖRG. Is this because of that runaway?

AGNES. It needn't concern you.

Silence.

JÖRG. We're forgetting – everything.

Silence.

I could rent one of those bigger units.

AGNES. Go.

It's not because of the money. You needn't worry about me. – And you can't keep clinging to me.

JÖRG. Why?

AGNES. I've been lying to you.

And now I haven't got time for this any more.

18. In Nelly's Bar

NELLY. Keep on drinking like that and the cleaning'll never catch up. The amount you owe.

YANNE. Haven't I got something to celebrate?

Being deported.

NELLY. Well. You'll be able to see your fiancée again.

YANNE. She won't recognise me. And if she does recognise me, she won't want to remember.

NELLY. What did you expect? That she'd wait for you till the end of time?

Silence.

YANNE. I've forgotten her too.

Silence.

Nelly. What am I going to do? I can't go back. Not with them on my conscience. Both of them.

NELLY. Are you to blame –

The old woman jumping off the bridge didn't surprise anyone.

She'll have had a reason.

And the Polish tobacconist – he's got a stone in his chest. Of tar. That's all.

YANNE. He's dying, Nelly. Dying.

And he won't see me.

Silence.

NELLY. So you don't want to go back?

YANNE. You think I'm drinking for fun.

The war.

Yeah. Maybe I should go. It would be a way out.

NELLY. D'you think I'm letting you go with a slate the size you've got?

YANNE. Not much else you can do.

NELLY. They can't deport you if you get married.

YANNE. Oh yeah.

NELLY. Think about it.

Silence. YANNE *understands.*

YANNE. I already practically stabbed one guy because he thought he could make a fool out of me. And man or woman makes no difference as far as I'm concerned.

NELLY (*suggestively*). Right. So stab me then.

Silence.

YANNE. I don't know what you have in mind for me.

NELLY. It's quite simple. You get proper papers. A room, food. And you can keep your tips. And you work here. For me. Not just cleaning. Waiter, the lot.

YANNE. Cheap labour in other words.

NELLY. It's better than the army.

Silence.

If it doesn't work out, we'll split up. Won't lose anything by it.

YANNE. A business arrangement.

NELLY. If that's what you want to call it.

Silence.

YANNE. Business business. Everyone's life is one long bill. A list of all the times we've sold ourselves. Over and over again. Till we're dead. And what for?

NELLY. A residence permit. A job. A bed. A little money.

YANNE. In a stranger's house.

Yes.

Why should I be any different?

NELLY. So. Something to celebrate.

YANNE. Nelly.

Here's to understanding each other –

NELLY. I never said anything about understanding.

Epilogue

The Dream about the Falcon

YANNE. I dreamt I was a falcon. The old guard had taken me
to his place. He'd taken off the chain that had tied me to the
rock; there was no need for it any more; I was too weak and
wretched to fly away. Death was in my eyes. What thought-
less demonstrations of strength I'd made when I was first
chained up; nothing could break my courage: if only my
wings could stretch as far as the vast strong sail that had
carried me for so long, I thought I wouldn't need to climb up
to the sky, because the sky would come to me. It would
swoop down, pick me up in its endless brilliant blue and
carry me off for ever. But that didn't happen. Nothing
happened, no matter how sharply my clamorous cries cut the
sky. They were shattered by the power of that silent space,
keeping all the answers to itself, and landed in another sea
somewhere, unheard.

Every time I tried to fly into the light, my body was pulled
back by the chain and crashed against the rock splattered
with feathers and bloody excrement. My foot was scabbed
and bleeding where the chain grabbed it. I was thin, my eyes
watered; my captors forced me to drink salt water and
laughed when the brine overran my torn beak and dribbled
its corrosive tongues into my open flesh to make my body
writhe.

They must have left me for dead – that was why one of the
guards, the oldest, could take me away one night to another
rock in his yard at home. He washed my feathers carefully
with a sponge, gently loosening the scabs. He brought me
water, clear, pure water, neither salty nor too cold, in a flat
bowl. But I was too weak to dip my beak in and drink. So
the old man scooped the water up with his hands and poured

it down my throat. He didn't smile, he talked quietly to himself, I didn't understand. Only one word stuck out from among the others like a thorn, it was painful for me to hear it. The old man kept coming night after night until I'd be waiting for him crouched on my rock not trembling. He'd give me the water dish and I'd drink it down greedily. Then I'd spray water over my wings and flick it with my beak over the old man's face. He didn't flinch though a smile would hide under a flicker of his eyelids. Again he'd talk to me, again very quietly, but there was no mistake, again he'd say one word which struck me a short hot blow every time.

I spent the following days stretching and strengthening my muscles and sinews, making my wings supple again. At night, when the old man came, I would eat and drink while I watched him out of the corner of my eye. He stood there quite calmly and seemed to be waiting.

Then one night he put my food down and disappeared only to return unexpectedly at dawn. He looked out to sea for a long time, just like he had when I was held captive and he used to visit me on my rock.

The wind carried the cool salty smell of the sea up towards us, and the thin line between the sea and the sky seemed to widen into a gap and behind it was infinite light. The old man scooped the water up in his hands one last time and offered it to me. I drank hurriedly. The light beyond the line of the sea intensified. The old man stood before me and now I understood exactly what the word meant and my throat unleashed a hard bright cry. The old man took a couple of steps back until I looked at him and then he leant back against my rock till his head came to rest just in front of my claws. I let out another clear and painful cry, then I grabbed the old man's collar securely in my beak and there it was, the fear that set my heart racing, but now it fired me and carried me, my wings rode broad and strong on the waves of the wind, the old man too spread out his arms and I carried him higher and higher towards the light that was shining at the edge of the sea and underneath us I could hear voices being carried up by the wind and with each beat of my heart they sang: SLOBODA SLOBODA. (*Freedom Freedom.*)

THE TABLE LAID

by Anna Langhoff

translated by David Spencer

Anna Langhoff was born in 1965 in East Berlin and comes from a theatre family. Her grandfather, Wolfgang Langhoff, was the director of the Deutsches Theater, Berlin, from 1946 to 1963. She worked as a director in Zurich and Hamburg and as dramaturg at the Schiller Theater, Berlin, before writing her first play *Transit Heimat: Gedeckte Tische* (*The Table Laid*), which premiered at the Deutsches Theater, Berlin, in 1994 and has since been translated into French, Dutch and Russian. Langhoff's other plays include *Schmidt Deutschland der Rosa Riese* (Berliner Ensemble, 1995), *Frieden Frieden* (1996) and *Antigone und ich mein Schatz bleib hier* (1997).

The Table Laid was first presented in English as a rehearsed reading as part of the *New German Voices* season in the Theatre Upstairs on 5 Octoher 1995 with the following cast:

Lajos Brocak, *a Romanian Gypsy*	Pip Donaghy
Maria Brocak, *his wife, Romanian*	Carole Hayman
Anna Brocak, *their daughter, Romanian*	Louisa Milwood Haigh
Galina Duvidowitsch, *Azerbaijani*	Saskia Reeves
Michail Duvidowitsch, *her husband, Ukrainian*	Dominic Grant
Pjotr Pajewskij, *a Russian of Ausslieder birth*	Nicholas Jones
Ljudmila Pajewskaja, *his wife, a Russian of German origin*	
	Barbara Ewing
Elena Mailovic, *Croatian, from 'Yugoslavia'*	Anabelle Apsion
Vedran Mailovic, *her husband, Serbian, from 'Yugoslavia'*	
	Razaaq Adoti
Wadek Kuzciwski, *Polish*	David Bamber
Frau Mertel, *German, a social worker*	Penny Downie

Director   Lindsay Posner
Translator   David Spencer

The first workshop presentation of the play in English took place at the Arts Depot in London on 7 April 1997 with the following cast:

Lajos Brocak	Fred Pearson
Maria Brocak	Julie Legrand
Anna Brocak	Galit Hershkovitz
Galina Duvidowitsch	Saskia Reeves
Michail Duvidowitsch	Simon Kunz
Pjotr Pajewski	Boris Isarov
Ljudmila Pajewskaja	Annette Badland
Elena Mailovic	Brana Bajic
Vedran Mailovic	Boris Boskovic
Wadek Kuzciwski	Karl Johnson
Frau Mertel	Suzanne Burden

Director   Lindsay Posner
Translator   David Spencer
Designer   Joanna Parker

1

A refugee-hostel kitchen in present-day Germany.

A bare and dirty room. Neon-strip lighting on the ceiling. Tiles on the lower half of the walls. Several ovens, a large draining board, very basic and ugly tables and chairs. A large cupboard with a number of locked compartments. Some of the locks are clearly damaged.

One door leads to a corridor, the other into the yard. One window has a broken pane, through another we see part of the yard wall. On the wall – even though it has been painted over in a makeshift manner – the slogan 'ASYLANTEN RAUS!' can still be read.

The BROCAK *family at a table eat and converse in Romanian.*

Enter WADEK KUZCIWSKI.

WADEK KUZCIWSKI (*as in, 'I have to live here'*). Here?

The BROCAKS *continue eating, silently.*

WADEK KUZCIWSKI. It stink here, I tell you. How can someone cook coffee here? It make vomit.

MARIA BROCAK. This is drains. Always smell. Everything go rot.

WADEK KUZCIWSKI. Lovely Anna. What can we say? Nobody understanding. You not. Me not. The stink is getting stronger!

ANNA BROCAK. You no talk me that! You go my Father. Leave me alone.

WADEK KUZCIWSKI. OK. Just a word. But first. Good afternoon Anna.

LAJOS BROCAK. Naa! He crazy.

WADEK KUZCIWSKI. Your Gypo feed stink. What you got today? Oh? Horse meat. Or dog meat?

LAJOS BROCAK (*to* MARIA.) The food is good. (*To* WADEK.) You let us in peace!

WADEK KUZCIWSKI. Peace! That's good! Always noise! Screaming. Always music. Or childs crying. And top that. Everyday you mess the kitchen! (*Laughs.*) Peace? That's good. (*To* LAJOS.) I wait twenty carton cigarettes.

LAJOS BROCAK. Yeah yeah.

WADEK KUZCIWSKI. I wait to get them back. You hear me?

LAJOS BROCAK. What? Cigarette? I don't smoke.

WADEK KUZCIWSKI. Very funny. Good joke. Give me them back now. This now!

LAJOS BROCAK. I got nothing of you.

WADEK KUZCIWSKI. The bag. I give you four days ago. At night. Give it me or else . . .

LAJOS BROCAK. What or else? Four days ago? When police come look for illegal cigarette dealer. Come look for spirit and cigarette. *Collect evidence.* Then you give me cigarette?

WADEK KUZCIWSKI. Lend OK. Lend. You may hide.

LAJOS BROCAK. Ah? Hide! Illegal cigarette to sell on street. Yes?

WADEK KUZCIWSKI. Give back. I need them. I not have much time.

LAJOS BROCAK. I have nothing. But if you want look with police. *Collect evidence.*

WADEK KUZCIWSKI. I stand for this? From a Gypo? (*Wants to go.*) You don't do it this way. You don't do me this way.

LAJOS BROCAK. You want keep your Polack face? You shut your mouth now.

WADEK KUZCIWSKI. OK knife-man. You come on! You go more quickly back to shit Romania. There you belong anyway.

LAJOS *jumps up.*

MARIA BROCAK (*to* LAJOS). Sitting down. I feel sure bad things come. Look out Lajos. Don't move. Me is afraid. Something comes. Please calm. No speak.

LAJOS BROCAK. Yeah calm. Calm. (*As* LAJOS *sits.*) We will see.

MARIA BROCAK. All sign on walls and water go black. (*To* WADEK.) You. What you?

ANNA BROCAK (*to* WADEK). Not good. Not you. With us eating? Is good soup. Hot. (*Laughs.*) Very hot.

WADEK KUZCIWSKI (*irritated*). No. No thank you.

WADEK *puts water on an oven.*

ANNA BROCAK. It Lesco. I have cooked.

WADEK KUZCIWSKI. When you one-time cook Bigosz Anna. But *that* I don't eat. You can't help it. It's what you taught. Some shit this Romanian mess.

ANNA BROCAK. No. Not Romanian. Is us from. Is famous from taste. Must fry garlic and onion until brown. Then peppers in. Green red. Tomato and cook. Cook with pepper when all thick. Little water. Some cut bit sausage. More cook. Then good.

Enter LJUDMILA PAJEWSKAJA. LJUDMILA*'s cupboard compartment has been broken into and emptied.*

LJUDMILA PAJEWSKAJA. Again. Gone again. This is ridiculous. No really. How can anyone coping with this?

WADEK KUZCIWSKI (*at the* BROCAKS: *provocative*). Things gone again?

LJUDMILA PAJEWSKAJA. It's a disgrace!

ANNA BROCAK. What?

LJUDMILA PAJEWSKAJA. Here is no life!

WADEK KUZCIWSKI. No. Not with *those* people.

LJUDMILA PAJEWSKAJA (*at* WADEK, *bewildered*). What you saying? (*At the door. Calls.*) Pjotr! Pjotr! Come here. Someone has stolen again.

WADEK KUZCIWSKI. Yeah. You must cope with *Auslanders* here.

MARIA BROCAK. You silence! Understanding? We no badder. Not take nothing. All food is us.

LAJOS BROCAK. They crazy Maria. All crazy.

Enter PJOTR PAJEWSKIJ.

PJOTR PAJEWSKIJ. *Sto eto?* What is the matter Mila? What are you shouting about? Calm yourself.

LJUDMILA PAJEWSKAJA. The cupboard. Here. Broken. Someone has taken everything. Meat. Eggs. Flour. Even the *Piroschnoje*.

PJOTR PAJEWSKIJ. It's *Kuchen* Mila. In German it's called *Kuchen*.

LJUDMILA PAJEWSKAJA. Good *Kuchen*. But gone.

PJOTR PAJEWSKIJ. You do want to learn?

LJUDMILA PAJEWSKAJA. Yes yes cake. But gone.

PJOTR PAJEWSKIJ (*a general announcement*). I am now forced to complain to the hostel authorities. Someone here is stealing from everyone.

WADEK KUZCIWSKI. Ha! *Someone!*

PJOTR PAJEWSKIJ. What shall I cook? What! It's all a disgrace.

WADEK KUZCIWSKI. *Someone* who has more than us. (*To* PJOTR.) For childs they get money. Lot of money.

LAJOS BROCAK. Lot of children is lot of hunger. All need shoe. Trouser. Coat.

PJOTR PAJEWSKIJ (*to* LJUDMILA). Then you can't cook anything.

WADEK KUZCIWSKI. No one know reason why? Anyway
they go beg everyday. Even the little girls. At night in the
*Restauracia. Please please. Something for baby and my sick
Mama. We big hunger.* Ha!

LJUDMILA PAJEWSKAJA *(to* PJOTR: *childish defiance).*
I am hungry!

WADEK KUZCIWSKI *(for* PJOTR). Beggars. Gypos.
Thieves. Murderers. With like of *this* you'll have your
experience. I know. Peasants from the end of the world . . .

PJOTR PAJEWSKIJ *(for* WADEK: *dismissive).* I am not
listening.

WADEK KUZCIWSKI *(for* PJOTR.) I want to help because
you and me. We not that sort. But you rather ignore me?
Me. Your friend. Wadek. OK. You wait. Wait and . . .

PJOTR PAJEWSKIJ *(at* WADEK). That's enough!

WADEK KUZCIWSKI. *Doswidanja.*

   Exit WADEK KUZCIWSKI.

PJOTR PAJEWSKIJ *(before* LJUDMILA *can answer).* Don't
talk to him. This is not a public meeting.

ANNA BROCAK. You can buy from us. For what it cost.

LJUDMILA PAJEWSKAJA. Buy! Buy! I own nothing to buy.

ANNA BROCAK. Yes . . .

LAJOS BROCAK. We also not.

ANNA BROCAK. If Duvidowitsch help 'til Monday? You
from same country.

LJUDMILA PAJEWSKAJA. Yes. If . . .

PJOTR PAJEWSKIJ. Definitely not them. And on top of that.
We're not in need of help. Not help. Only our rights.

LAJOS BROCAK. Crazy! *(To* MARIA.) Come on.

   Exit MARIA BROCAK.

LJUDMILA PAJEWSKAJA *(to* PJOTR). In room we still have boiled potatoes. The bowl is on top of the books. You get it?

PJOTR PAJEWSKIJ. Potatoes . . . on books . . . God.

Exit PJOTR PAJEWSKIJ.

LAJOS BROCAK. Give her flour Anna. Or else she cries more.

Exit LAJOS BROCAK.

ANNA *clears the table, sets flour before* LJUDMILA, *starts to wash up.*

LJUDMILA PAJEWSKAJA. Thank you. You will definitely get it back.

LJUDMILA *tips flour onto the table, adds water, a pinch of salt, kneads the dough. As she speaks the kneading grows harder and harder. as if the dough were to blame for everything.*

LJUDMILA PAJEWSKAJA *(into space)*. Just go they said. Go happily to Germany. Yeah yeah. There everyone does well. They're not like they were before. Very friendly. They help refugees. And your husband has a German grandfather. That's good. Straightaway they give you a house and work. You will be like Germans. No difference . . . But what? How? This here is not Germany. It is worse than shared housing. Worse than the central sewage works! What a Germany. Yugoslavs. Romanians. Russians. Poles. Jews. *(Laughs.)* Even Jews. In Germany. All lumped together. Cats in a sack. Waiting. Always waiting. For what? Beautiful fate. No permission to stay. You can't go. Just living. Surviving.

There is work. Houses. *Kindergartens.* Peace. But for whom? Not for us. Really beautiful Germany!

ANNA BROCAK. They not like that.

LJUDMILA PAJEWSKAJA. Pardon?

ANNA BROCAK. German. Not friendly. Ever. Every bad for us.

LJUDMILA PAJEWSKAJA. Probably . . . probably . . .

ANNA BROCAK. Definitely. When we come at nights. Polices scream bad and shove us. Sending back. We three times cross border. Always in good and dark. It was rains. But Police just bring back. Say. *Asylum? No!* Four time no one see us. So we go next town. At last being in Germany. Where should be rich and living for all. First we tired. Sleep in waited room of train station. Baby crying. Men not stay with us. Go look hostel like this. Look relatives.

LJUDMILA PAJEWSKAJA. In the station. With the children!?

ANNA BROCAK. They scream. *Raus! Raus! Auslander Raus! Fuck off.* We do nothing. All fear. But they beat us. Shouting loud. Big loud. My sister bleeds . . .

LJUDMILA PAJEWSKAJA. I'm sorry.

ANNA BROCAK. Young men with no hair holding long stick. All on feets soldier boots. They laughing. Pushing. Shoving mine. Police come late. Come very slowly . . . touch us with rubber gloves . . .

LJUDMILA PAJEWSKAJA. Police? The same everywhere. Listen. You may not show you are from Romania. And run away. Don't stand still. That's how it is. There's no decency . . . Dough is ready now. You see. Flour. Water. Salt. Simple. The filling must on the middle. And then close together. Like a bag.

ANNA BROCAK. Meat? Yes?

LJUDMILA PAJEWSKAJA. Meat will do. But I like more potatoes. Onions. And curd cheese.

ANNA *takes two onions from her compartment and peels them.*

ANNA BROCAK. You and your husband. Why coming here?

LJUDMILA PAJEWSKAJA. We are from Minsk. But his parents are from Germany. *Yes* he says. *Home again.*

ANNA BROCAK. Mother and father German?

LJUDMILA PAJEWSKAJA. Yes. Russian German. Because of that is possible *they* let us stay. A hope. At home all is poor. Living one flat together with other family. No bath. No space. Until there is better. Am I *Babuschka* . . . Old woman.

ANNA BROCAK. Live together with other. Here like too. (*Laughs.*)

LJUDMILA PAJEWSKAJA. Yes no. Now. One time I shall better life . . . And you?

ANNA BROCAK. We live in small town at edge. No heating. Dirty. Cramp. Little food. Stink. We all time used to it. But now people hunting us like animal hunt animal. Many dead. Everyone can be dangerous. Ceaucescu at last go. But nothing better. Not for us.

LJUDMILA PAJEWSKAJA. Now you must frying the onions.

ANNA *puts a frying pan on the oven, spoons in oil.*

ANNA BROCAK. I bake pastry totally same. With peppers. And meat. Our food is good. If enough. My brother always says. In Romania everything tasting better.

LJUDMILA PAJEWSKAJA (*fries onions*). Should go brown. Golden onions. (ANNA *and* LJUDMILA *laugh.*) That's how it is. Everywhere bad . . . I wish to eat Pelmeni. In a small flat with white curtains. One room. Maybe two . . . and invite the neighbours. Possibly . . . or not? No? At home our neighbours. You could speak with them. Laugh and argue. But here . . . These people are porters. Winter sits in their eyes. All squatting at the entrance. Lying in wait grinning. Showing rubber stamps . . . Like best to stay alone at house. I and I with me . . .

ANNA BROCAK. A room for mine. One for sister. Such good. At home always dust. Black dust. But something is different. My father says. *Here is good. Romania shit.* But I think back.

LJUDMILA PAJEWSKAJA. Onion. Potato. And curd cheese. Must stick like porridge. Bit of pepper . . . (*At door.*) If only he is coming.

ANNA BROCAK. *Tut.* Room. Room . . .

LJUDMILA PAJEWSKAJA. Where you grow up is always a place to hide. Or does your fiancé wait?

ANNA BROCAK. No. No. But at home is a . . . something like . . . I don't know.

Enter PJOTR PAJEWSKI.

PJOTR PAJEWSKI (*a bowl*). I've brought curdled cheese too. You see. Everything is okay.

LJUDMILA PAJEWSKAJA. Everything is here.

ANNA BROCAK (*cheerful*). My mother will still . . .

PJOTR PAJEWSKI (*unfriendly*). We would like to eat in peace. Please.

LJUDMILA *doesn't look up from the potatoes. cheese, and onions, which she mixes into a lump. She then fills the pieces of dough and puts water on the oven to boil. She's* over-busy *throughout.*

ANNA BROCAK. Oh.

ANNA *looks furtively at* LJUDMILA.

Exit ANNA BROCAK.

PJOTR PAJEWSKI. I will not have that, Mila. I will not have her in my house.

LJUDMILA PAJEWSKAJA. This is hostel. Hostel kitchen. Not your house.

PJOTR PAJEWSKI. Even so.

LJUDMILA PAJEWSKAJA. She gave us onion and flour.

PJOTR PAJEWSKI. Very possibly your onions.

LJUDMILA PAJEWSKAJA. I don't think . . .

PJOTR PAJEWSKI. They are uneducated. Certainly not clean.

LJUDMILA PAJEWSKAJA. And you don't like the Pole either. He spoke to you . . .

PJOTR PAJEWSKI. Such people aren't company for us. Not even in this predicament. Have you ever had something to do with his sort? Ever? No! So why now? Why give him attention. If before you hadn't even seen such a man? Swindling people on the streets. Tax-free cigarettes and his cup and pea game. Which he of course always wins. His friends deal in stolen cars. All the time he tries to drag me into his business. In the end. Because of such crooks we would not be allowed to live here. How should we decide? When not even you separate and decide.

LJUDMILA PAJEWSKAJA. Rubbish. They were always against strangers. Yesterday. Today. Suddenly again they want rid of us. But who now will slave for Germany? Perhaps you. Perhaps we should . . .

PJOTR PAJEWSKI. Oh what. Politics. You and I. We're not like the refugees. Or the Poles. We simply don't have these worries.

LJUDMILA PAJEWSKAJA. Your German face is Russian for Germans. And you are poor. You understand? Poor. That worser than sick. Your origins are forgotten. They all screamed as if they must hunger. *Turks Raus! Poles Raus! Romanians Raus! Russians Raus!* And I am not like you. I have no German grandfather to show. (LJUDMILA *cries*.) At night. Even in my sleep they scream. *Raus Ljudmila Pajewskaja. Get out of our ordered separate sleep. Get out of our night. Why are you still living? Why do you beg from us? What do you want?*

PJOTR PAJEWSKI. Stop that, Mila. Please.

LJUDMILA PAJEWSKAJA (*shouts. almost sobs*). *Raus. Fuck off Russian. Raus. Raus. Raus!*

PJOTR PAJEWSKI. It's because of this I have written to the authorities. We can't live here like this. I wrote of my grandfather. His story. That my father spoke German. They suffered under Stalin! Oh yes. You know that. I have told you enough. The contempt. The oppression. Always the same insults. *You Fascists.* And all that. If they are not giving me a German passport then good. But locking us up

here. That's not right! Not justice! You too want to leave
this cold stupid Russia. You too don't want to stay a lifetime
among those people. Fighting one another over each piece
of meat. Their place to live or a few roubles more. Until
they are full and thick. And the rest are hungry and also
thick. Wait until we are used to it. Here is the centre of
culture. Humanism. Civilisation and advancement. Soon we
will belong to it. We must learn. You must.

LJUDMILA *takes the last* Pelmeni *from the water and puts
it in the bowl.*

LJUDMILA PAJEWSKAJA. Learn. Learn. What still learn?

PJOTR PAJEWSKI (*at the door*). Here comes our Jewess.

LJUDMILA PAJEWSKAJA. What?

PJOTR PAJEWSKI. Here comes the Poor-Jew-Woman. You
don't know?! They had to leave the *soooooo* anti-semitic
Russia, and return to their Promised Land. But then they
came here. That is really laughable.

LJUDMILA PAJEWSKAJA. You are very much the German.

Enter GALINA DUVIDOWITSCH.

GALINA DUVIDOWITSCH. *Sdrasdwuij.*

LJUDMILA PAJEWSKAJA *murmurs something
incomprehensible.*

PJOTR PAJEWSKI. Good afternoon.

GALINA *takes bread, smoked herrings and margarine from
the cupboard. She puts them on the table.*

LJUDMILA PAJEWSKAJA. So. Ready.

PJOTR PAJEWSKI. Then let's go.

PJOTR *picks up the bowl.* LJUDMILA, *behind* GALINA's
back, takes a spoonful of margarine and puts it in the bowl.

LJUDMILA PAJEWSKAJA. *Charascho.* Now it will be real
tasty.

Exit LJUDMILA PAJEWSKAJA *and* PJOTR PAJEWSKI.

GALINA *smears slices of white bread with margarine.*

GALINA DUVIDOWITSCH (*laughs*). A journalist goes to Red Square in *Moskau*. He asks a woman. *Is there anti-semitism in, Russia?* The woman shakes her head. Stares at him and says. *In Russia there is nothing.*

Enter VEDRAN MAILOVIC.

VEDRAN MAILOVIC. There you are yes. I demand that you pay attention to your son.

GALINA DUVIDOWITSCH (*her line of thought broken*). Humm?

VEDRAN MAILOVIC. Your son. Always your son. My wife is pregnant.

GALINA DUVIDOWITSCH. Yeah and? Is that my boy's fault?

VEDRAN MAILOVIC. What? What! If he comes again. Then I not care. (*Indicates a blow to the ear.*) He gets this.

GALINA DUVIDOWITSCH. My God? Can no one have peace? Hit a child. A small child! What has he done.

VEDRAN MAILOVIC. What done? What! Always playing front of our door. Always loud. Boom boom boom. His ball against the wall. My wife must sleep.

GALINA DUVIDOWITSCH. So sleep. And nights? Whole night TV on. Screaming. Swearing. Door open. Door close. But my Aljoscha not allowed to play. (*Mimics* VEDRAN.) *My wife is pregnant.* Ha!

VEDRAN MAILOVIC. Listen you. It hard for Elena. We see news from home. More shooting. Then she cries and want go telephoning. But that senseless. No connection. Only costs lot of money. She is unhappy.

GALINA DUVIDOWITSCH. That is really very sad.

GALINA *and* VEDRAN *stare at each other.*

GALINA DUVIDOWITSCH. Yes and?

VEDRAN MAILOVIC. How?

GALINA DUVIDOWITSCH. What then?

VEDRAN MAILOVIC. Ja . . . Oh. Then she cries more and
shouts me. You have to understand. She is disturbed and
says I don't care about her family. I am Serbian. That
we are all the same gang. All murderers. Then I get
annoyed. My uncle was killed by Croatians. *Elena* I say.
Now that's . . .

GALINA DUVIDOWITSCH. Yeah yeah. We hear it. And
that's enough! Go back and fight your war but not here.
Not getting on our nerves. Maybe you kill each other?'
What a marriage! Poor baby will sometime have to tear
itself in two.

VEDRAN *slams the door.*

Exit VEDRAN MAILOVIC.

GALINA DUVIDOWITSCH (*calling after him*). Serb Croat.
What is that? What differences have you found. What is
your shit problem.

GALINA *sits at the table. Resigned, she rests her head in
her hand.*

Maybe you know? But how can I explain to my son. His
grandmother still wore a veil. Had both her arms covered to
her wrists even on the hottest of days. She understood no
Russian. In her house there was no water. She brought it
from the stream. Day by day. The buckets were heavy. But
then men came. And girls in light blouses. They laughed
loudly on the dust track. Shoes stained grey. The men
and the girls. They called a meeting in the village square.
Made speeches. Said. *Moscow is ruled by the working class.
It is revolution!* But Moscow was distant. My grandmother
hadn't noticed the revolution. Still. Everyone there knew.
That into dark kitchens. They would bring water and
electricity. *Women* called one girl. *Are like men. have the
same rights and the same duties. Woman can't flee from the
new age. No longer shall you wrap in veils to inhibit and
bind you.* The veils fell into the dust. *From now on.*
Laughed Grandmother. *Men must give birth in great pain.
Must bleed and be alone. Have the stillborn ripped from*

their guts. Must be ashamed and burn red rags in the oven
whilst no one looks. And all that. (Scornfully.) Imagine it.
All that with electricity, (Murmurs.) But the thing with the
veil is good. As my mother left the village electricity
arrived. On her deathbed Grandmother saw the flicker of
a naked bulb. *You see* she breathed. *There is light there.*
Mother worked in the factory. Married a lorry driver from
Kiew. My father told me. *Back then she sang like a bird.*
Later she stopped singing. Cursed him. More and more.
Croaking and tired. Then she drank. She wanted it better.
Better. But none of us knew what she meant by that. And
then when I married Michail I seldom visited my parents.
And then one time was the last time. Michail's a good man.
He often brought me fruit. Scarce things. Perfume even for
my birthday. He didn't care about politics. But now. He
broods. Now he hates Jews. And he hates them because he
is one. Sadly he had a friend with connections. False
documents. Michail gave the car for them. Then we were
both Jews. An old car would have done. Unbelievable.
He's not even circumcised. *Pow.* Car here. *Pow.* Jew there.
Then we waited for emigration forms. It didn't take long.
Everything will be better said Michail. When we got to
Israel he gave the last of my money for more false
documents. So that we could travel quickly to Germany.
Yes. It has got better. Yes. Better . . . Suddenly he washes
himself daily. He soaps and scrubs but Jew stays. Jew
doesn't want to go away. He can't stand Jew on his skin.
And they come from their Community Centre to help. He
can't stand it. He stares sideways like a trained dog. Afraid
he's too similar. At night. When Michail sleeps. And the
mirrored moon stares. I remember a thin covering of clay.
Warm Pitta. I hear the warning song of the cicadas. The
lambs cry. I smell their shorn hair. Washed and unspun I see
it spread before the hut door. Drying in the sun. But this
was never my life. It's Grandmother's dream calling me.
I hear her hum. From under piles of patchwork quilts where
she lay me. Everything smells of animal. Of human. Of
soup and corn. Secretly I dream. A fugitive. Face hid
beneath a veil of fake skin. No one knows. But secretly
I dream. Cocooned in lies. Me. Conceived in a village's

still. Born on the way. Me from the city of Kiew. Crossing
the *Kaukasus* in mother's belly. Me. A stranger in memories
of *Aserbaidschan*. Stranger on every border . . . It'll be
better . . . One time I'll be home. One time I'll see others
with owners' eyes. Think. This place is mine. I belong here.
Here belongs to me. And all here are guests. Strangers in
my separate silence. In my place. I want. One time. Not
to see stools in strange living rooms. Or pictures of other
people's parents. I want don't to ask. *Where's this memory
waiting? Where's my security?* I will want just once in this
maze to find a familiar region. But you can't search for
the spot from where you come. To journey out of myself?
How to do that?

Enter FRAU MERTEL.

FRAU MERTEL. Good afternoon Frau Duvidowitsch.

GALINA DUVIDOWITSCH. Good afternoon. Good
afternoon.

FRAU MERTEL. Is everything in order?

GALINA DUVIDOWITSCH. But naturally. Life's sugar!
Everything tasteful and sweetened. And in order. Above all
in order.

FRAU MERTEL. What? I see. I'm glad. (*A little irritated.*)
Frau Pajewskaja tells me that *again* a cupboard was broken
open.

GALINA DUVIDOWITSCH. Never? There's always
something.

FRAU MERTEL. I hope that will change. My idea of having a
meal together should smooth out the difficulties. At least
you can cook communally. Get to know each other and each
other's food. We have ten different nationalities in the
Hostel.

GALINA DUVIDOWITSCH. Yeah. Just no niggers or Indians.
But actually we are *all* refugees. If we make ourselves very
tiny and very quiet. Then you might give us sweetie?

FRAU MERTEL. You're in a bad mood are you? Have you all discussed your plans for Sunday night?

GALINA DUVIDOWITSCH. Who?

FRAU MERTEL. All of you. I thought you'd planned something.

GALINA DUVIDOWITSCH. What should we plan? My husband won't really come.

FRAU MERTEL. He'll come as soon as we're all sitting together. I'm really happy I managed to get the money released. The food's to be delivered today. I think it will bring you all a little closer. You as a Jew. You must think exactly like me. Animosity toward different kinds of people is the beginning of racism. Violence. Even amongst yourselves.

GALINA DUVIDOWITSCH. You mean well but what is use to us? It doesn't change the problem.

FRAU MERTEL. We'll see. A small step's better than nothing.

Enter ELENA MAILOVIC.

ELENA MAILOVIC. You . . . You! What you say my husband?! What we done? Your son is always noise making. Why insulting my baby? What. Poor child? What not Serb? Not Croat? Goes broken?

GALINA DUVIDOWITSCH. Shut your mouth yes. I'm not speaking to you.

ELENA MAILOVIC. And we make war. We in bad Yugoslavia! But why that? You are to blame. You Russians! Whole trouble starts with your shit country!

GALINA DUVIDOWITSCH (*laughs*). Sweetheart I'm a Jew. Complain elsewhere.

FRAU MERTEL. What's the matter now? Speak reasonably to each other.

ELENA MAILOVIC. Frau. These people thinking only of self. Always in kitchen. Never wash dishes. Everything dirt. In toilet child make mess. He play on stairs. Mother not care. Loud. So loud. My head caving in from this devil.

GALINA DUVIDOWITSCH. And them? Screaming every night. Not turn TV off. Disturbing the sleep. Crazy couple. In the day. Kiss kiss. And holding hands. My darling here. Little sweet heart there. Put in their room alone. They mount a circus for the whole of the hostel.

FRAU MERTEL. But the child really shouldn't play in the hostel. It's not allowed. She should go with him to a playground.

GALINA DUVIDOWITSCH (*screams*). Who plays? Where? She's lying. But her husband works illegally. You see that's how it is. They cheat the state and are big mouthed.

Enter MICHAIL DUVIDOWITSCH.

MICHAIL *carries a child's ball.*

MICHAIL DUVIDOWITSCH (*to* MERTEL). Ah . . . Yes . . .

ELENA MAILOVIC. Such meanness! My husband here. Not working somewhere. He here. You can come see.

GALINA DUVIDOWITSCH. Yeah. Here now. To-day. (*To* MERTEL.) Sat-ur-day.

MICHAIL DUVIDOWITSCH (*to* GALINA). Stop it. Be quiet.

GALINA DUVIDOWITSCH. Don't mix. Go drinking. Thank you. How you stand by your wife. (*Screams.*) And give the ball here. Where is Aljoscha!? Why you take his ball?

ELENA MAILOVIC (*to* MERTEL.) Now you see. The manners of a goat. Even with her own husband,

MICHAIL DUVIDOWITSCH. We don't need your opinion. Could be I should be deaf? I not! Your screams know the whole house.

GALINA DUVIDOWITSCH. There you hear her.

FRAU MERTEL. Stop this nonsense now. You all must be a bit more considerate with one another. Surely that can't be so difficult!

ELENA MAILOVIC. You only talk. Always talk.

Exit ELENA MAILOVIC.

GALINA DUVIDOWITSCH (*to herself*). Not *so* difficult. She
should live here. One kitchen. One washroom. Everything
disgusting. No single square foot of my own! I thought here
wasn't socialist! But no. Social services. Immigration
police. Court. Lawyer. Housing office. Forms. Certificates.
Confirmation. Wait. Waiting. A stamp's missing. Wait . . .
Worse than Russia.

MICHAIL DUVIDOWITSCH. I can't hear it any more. All the
time. Day night. Talking. Why away. Why here. Why not
stay to home . . . Blahblah. Crying. Blahblah. Why? Why!

GALINA DUVIDOWITSCH. Yes why. For this here?

MICHAIL DUVIDOWITSCH. Yes. For this here. And my
fault. Are you happy. You are the only one who can't stand
it here. Only you have it hard. And my fault.

GALINA DUVIDOWITSCH (*to* MERTEL). What's that
supposed to be. A free country? Here people stick to farms
like flies on flypaper. I am a fly. I am stuck Michail on this
sweet syrup. And thrashing around doesn't help. Just sticks
more. What for? (*To* MERTEL.) What do you lock us up
here for?

FRAU MERTEL. But Frau Duvidowitsch I'm not to blame.
I can't do anything about it. I try my best.

GALINA DUVIDOWITSCH. Yes of course. I'm sorry. It
just . . . just slipped out. My meal is er. Ready.

GALINA *lifts her plate to go.*

MICHAIL DUVIDOWITSCH (*to* GALINA). I'll fetch
Aljoscha.

GALINA DUVIDOWITSCH. What? No. I call myself.

Exit GALINA DUVIDOWITSCH.

MICHAIL DUVIDOWITSCH *(to* MERTEL). Yes . . . Sorry.
I . . . But even so we . . . We Jews. You understand. We have

right here to live better. Be treated better by you. Because
we . . . Whatever.

Exit MICHAIL DUVIDOWITSCH.

MERTEL *stands alone in the kitchen. She washes her
hands. Disgusted, she doesn't use the dirty towel.*

Enter ANNA BROCAK.

FRAU MERTEL. Oh. Anna.

ANNA BROCAK. I look you.

FRAU MERTEL. Yes? What is it?

ANNA BROCAK. They always us vouchers give on social
office. No money.

FRAU MERTEL. Anna. The vouchers are worth the same as
money. Except you can't buy cigarettes or alcohol with
them.

ANNA BROCAK. That's why? But persons stare so. Me is
ashamed. And . . .

FRAU MERTEL. And?

ANNA BROCAK. I can't explain. At market or in small shops
not want take vouchers.

FRAU MERTEL. OK er. Monday. I'll phone your clerk.
Perhaps he'll listen to me.

ANNA BROCAK. You speak him yes?

FRAU MERTEL. It's out of my control. But I'll try to explain
your problem to him.

Enter WADEK KUZCIWSKI.

WADEK *has a black eye. He holds a half-full spirits bottle.*

WADEK KUZCIWSKI. Ah? Our Miss Kindergarten. You're
there. Come here. Come here. Care a bit about me.
(*Laughs.*) You not very beautiful. Bit pale. Like a maggot
maybe. But doesn't matter. Eh? Anna *is* beautiful. I miss
love. You know. Love is very important.

FRAU MERTEL. You're not allowed to drink in common areas. And stop this tasteless nonsense. If you don't like me. Stay out of my way.

WADEK KUZCIWSKI. Out of way? But you're sitting in my kitchen. (*Short laugh.*) In my kitchen. That's good! Come *Boschina*. Take a sip.

WADEK *tries to put the bottle to* ANNA*'s mouth.*

ANNA BROCAK. Not. Not.

WADEK KUZCIWSKI. Go Anna. Don't stare at me. You not understand.

FRAU MERTEL. Stop this crap. Imagine someone behaved like that with your wife?

WADEK KUZCIWSKI. My wife is a whore! Left me. And why? Because in your country. I not find work do. No work. No work. But *you* is sympathy. You me cheer up.

FRAU MERTEL. You vanish now before I become unpleasant.

WADEK KUZCIWSKI. In truth you are unpleasant.

FRAU MERTEL. That's enough!

ANNA, *alarmed, goes to the door but stays there.*

ANNA BROCAK. Stop it, Wadek! Come on. Go to park.

WADEK *stares at* MERTEL. *It looks like he'll go. He suddenly spins back.*

WADEK KUZCIWSKI. You whore! Pig! All pigs. I'll kill you all. You lie of a woman. Go fuck off your own home.

WADEK *throws the bottle. It misses* MERTEL. ANNA *starts to cry.*

Exit ANNA BROCAK.

WADEK KUZCIWSKI. Shit! It's all shit! I smash everything to bits! I'll kill you. (*To* MERTEL.) Kill you. You.

Enter PJOTR PAJEWSKI.

FRAU MERTEL. Now I'm calling the police.

PJOTR PAJEWSKI. They are already there. Just go outside.

FRAU MERTEL. What? What is it?

PJOTR PAJEWSKI. What should it be? It's the weekend
again . . . Uneducated people. Primitive. *Auslanders* . . .

FRAU MERTEL. What?

PJOTR PAJEWSKI. The Romanians. Romanians against the
Yugoslavs. I don't know what for. Someone's been stabbed.
The police are there. Come on. You can even see blood.

FRAU MERTEL. Every Saturday. I want to pull my hair out!

Exit FRAU MERTEL.

WADEK KUZCIWSKI. I'm idiot. At home family waits. Who
comes back?

PJOTR PAJEWSKI. How would I know?

WADEK KUZCIWSKI. Yeah and you? I won't live in Poland.

PJOTR PAJEWSKI. I must go.

WADEK KUZCIWSKI. Everyone needs a place. (PJTOR
stares poker-faced at WADEK.) I want talk. At the end you
give the answer. You hear. Over that screaming?

PJOTR PAJEWSKI. That doesn't interest me. Not only that . .
Frau Mertel is there to attend to it.

Exit PJOTR PAJEWSKI.

WADEK KUZCIWSKI. And me? Me forgotten very quick.
Call police . . . Bad Wadek . . . Yeah? Police? Nothing.
Nothing. Where those police? *Forgotten.* Not important.
Wadek not important . . . (*Calls.*) Anna! She's run too.

WADEK *sits, slumps on the table and cries.*

Blackout.

2

Sunday afternoon. There are more chairs in the kitchen than
Saturday afternoon. On the tables are boxes containing food,
tins, fresh vegetables, oil, salt, spices, meat etc.

LAJOS *sits next to* MARIA. *She prepares the filling for stuffed*
vine leaves.

MARIA BROCAK. We're all black. Luckless and luckless. Do
you hear me Lajos? We should go back. Back. Oh yeah. But
back where? There's no escape. Do you hear Lajos? Night
on night shines a lantern. Watches us. Watches our *dreams.*
I dream too much. I lay an embroidered cloth over the
cupboard. Beautiful. Colourful. Cramped between cupboard
bed and walls. Out in the yard. I sit on the steps. My skirt
hangs between my legs to the floor. The children sit. Press
their warm hands on stone. I sew bead after bead to the
seams of scarves. *These are for Anna's wedding* our sons
laugh. *But what wedding.* They throw the scarves into the
air. Hold blonde girls in their arms. Our sons laugh. Sit under
giant wheels. In roller coasters. Shoot imitation roses. Drive
wrecked cars. They sing. But in their bellies are tears. They
remember beauties from home. In the evening I let down
my hair. Stand lost at the window. Anna hands trembling.
Smoothes bedclothes half sewn with yesterday's ornaments.

Waiting for the wedding. Waiting for blood. I'm freezing.
Barefoot on cold linoleum. All alone at the blackboard.
Beside the German teacher. Stiff fingered. Letter for letter.
I copy her. *HERTZ. Heart* in German. What use is such a
word? I want to write the address of my sister on an
envelope. Put my name in the right box on a form. I don't
need to learn more. *Stone* says Anna in her sleep. She
writes songs on paper. Draws black lines on the tabletop.
Home is . . . The teacher writes on her board. *Home is*

where the heart is. I laugh until I can't laugh. Sit in the yard. Stare at the cloth's pattern. Hopscotch. Call the children back from the wall. *Home is* . . . Heaven and hell! Who ever reads that's a stranger. What should I tell the children? Our sons? I am their mother. I should tell them something. I should? I don't find the right word. They fly from my arms. Fat pigeons limp behind the rubbish bins. Cruelly pecking words from dirt. Swallowing them instantly. Anna cries. Words become raffle tickets. One must be the right one. We're all black and soulless. They didn't leave home with us. But wait. Wait there. Alone like ghosts.

LAJOS BROCAK. I know Maria. I know all that.

Enter ELENA MAILOVIC *and* VEDRAN MAILOVIC.

The MAILOVICS *begin to prepare their food for the meal.*

ELENA MAILOVIC. I have to. Whatever. I have to think of it.

VEDRAN MAILOVIC. *What?*

ELENA MAILOVIC. I can't think of anything else.

VEDRAN MAILOVIC. Yes but what?

ELENA MAILOVIC. I say way I want to.

VEDRAN MAILOVIC. Yes. But what?

ELENA MAILOVIC. What. What? You always question. Like you don't think. The Serbs let whole town starve. That's truth. In our villages? Slaughter. They kill *children.*

VEDRAN MAILOVIC. They're no worse than any others. It's a war for *life*. For days. Hours of life.

ELENA MAILOVIC. Even war has laws. But they not care. Not know shame.

VEDRAN MAILOVIC. What do you know? In the news here they show only pictures for the Croatians. Show always only what terrible Serbian soldiers again do. Serbs are inhumane. Serbs communist murderers. Serbs big danger. But the face of the Croatia they don't show. They're good people. Always *were*. Have also back then helped the German fascists killing.

ELENA MAILOVIC. Who are *they?* Who says that? Serbians are cruel. Serbians are brutal. All. They against peace.

VEDRAN MAILOVIC. Me.

ELENA MAILOVIC. Not you. Not every one. But most.

LAJOS BROCAK. Crazy. A crazy war without sense.

VEDRAN MAILOVIC (*resigned, for himself*). The sense of this war is the victory of its brutality. And . . .

Enter PJOTR PAJEWSKI.

PJOTR PAJEWSKI *seems to be looking for his wife.*

VEDRAN MAILOVIC. We'll ask Herr Pajewski. He's educated and knows.

ELENA MAILOVIC. A Russian. He will talk you is right.

VEDRAN MAILOVIC. So what. I ask. (*To* PJOTR.) Excuse me a moment. I'd like to have your opinion.

PJOTR PAJEWSKI. Pardon? Do you mean me?

VEDRAN MAILOVIC. Yes yes. My wife and I argue again. She doesn't knew the truth of this war. But I say Croatians to be very guilty. Only German news claims always different.

ELENA MAILOVIC. We want only freedom and own land.

PJOTR PAJEWSKI (*absent-minded*). Yes. Yes . . . What? What kind of freedom madam?

ELENA MAILOVIC. What a question! Freedom from *socialism.* Good life . . . to buy things . . . Freedom. (*To* VEDRAN.) But you. Fighting. Fighting. Fighting.

VEDRAN MAILOVIC. Yes of course. Alone. All alone. But *alone* we can't make war.

PJOTR PAJEWSKI. Excuse me. That's all politics. But you want to live don't you? Live here. Find a reason to be happy. Inner purpose. The world's being divided anew now.

Go with the times. Your old values laws are too useless to miss. Learn. Learn to forget. Good German. A profession. Prepare your future. And think of your child. These are your worries. And not pictures from the television. Toss away this medieval land like useless rubbish, Be happy rid of it. To be here. Without civil war.

ELENA MAILOVIC. We are not here. We only seem so. But when must we go back?

PJOTR PAJEWSKI. Scratch this rash from your skin or else . . .

VEDRAN MAILOVIC. But . . .

PJOTR PAJEWSKI. Yugoslavia! Pah! Why bother? An under-developed destroyed country. Who cares. The scrap-yard of Europe. The beggar. Yugoslavia. Romania. Poland. Bulgaria . . . it's all uncivilised. It's foul. Simply rotten. Here history is made and decided. The future. Here in Germany freedom is being invented. And *you* don't decide how or for whom.

ELENA MAILOVIC (*uncomprehending*). What?

VEDRAN MAILOVIC. Ah. Hum . . . But . . .

PJOTR PAJEWSKI. My good man. I have to find my wife.

PJOTR PAJEWSKI *wants to go.*

ELENA MAILOVIC. Have you forgotten your home? Have you thrown away your mother like a . . . like something . . . that no one wants?

PJOTR PAJEWSKI. Home? What nonsense! My family. Yes. I respect them. Treasure them. My parents have always tried to give me all they could. Be a good example. But then a new General Secretary moves in to the Kremlin. Things change. And we were again slandered. Poverty stricken. And why? Because my *home* handles its victims as it suits it. They betray everyone. Home. (*Laughs.*) A coat of holes.

ELENA MAILOVIC. But there are memories . . .

PJOTR PAJEWSKI (*rough*). No. No. There are only circumstances. When they're bad. Everything's bad. And *memories* can't help. I have to go now . . .

Exit PJOTR PAJEWSKI.

ELENA MAILOVIC. I knew it. (*Contemptuously*.) A Russian.

Enter ANNA BROCAK.

ANNA *begins to help with preparations.*

ANNA BROCAK (*shows the Pittas*). Complete fresh. How is belly?

ELENA MAILOVIC (*dismissive*). Good. Good. All in order.

ANNA BROCAK. My mother know everything. At home she called by lot of women when pain comes, She tell. When baby come. My mother help.

ELENA MAILOVIC (*tries to hide her terror*). No no not. I go to hospital. Is clean there. And good Doctor too.

VEDRAN MAILOVIC (*embarrassed. Over-polite*) But thank you very much . . . anyway.

Enter FRAU MERTEL.

MERTEL *takes off her coat.*

FRAU MERTEL. Good afternoon everyone.

LAJOS BROCAK. Good day.

ELENA MAILOVIC. Have you *heard. Information?* We still wait. No letter comed.

FRAU MERTEL. It *can* take some time.

ELENA MAILOVIC. We go back. Must go back!? Saving me!

FRAU MERTEL. No. *Not.* Before a notification is issued you can't be deported.

ELENA MAILOVIC. But they have sent even families. Sent back to war.

FRAU MERTEL. I wrote *your letter* exactly as you told me. And in your condition . . . you really shouldn't be afraid. Above that. If permission to stay is granted. Your sister in law has guaranteed to pay your living costs. That's very positive.

VEDRAN MAILOVIC. Yes. Please writing everything for Police. For us is impossible life. With the Croats they hunt me. And my people not want Elena. Not only war. Hate too. Always hate.

FRAU MERTEL. I've mentioned it all. You've probably the best circumstances. Especially your mixed marriage. That makes everything more difficult. And now they can't even fly you out. Since the situation gets worse daily. (*Radiating confidence and cheer.*) This war is turning into genocide. It's obvious.

Enter GALINA DUVIDOWITSCH.

GALINA DUVIDOWITSCH. This is what we have put up with! Such a mess. Who'll clean up then? Not my husband!

FRAU MERTEL. How's your son, Herr Brocak?

LAJOS BROCAK. OK. Not bad. A knife scratch. No disaster.

FRAU MERTEL. I'm afraid there'll be problems.

LAJOS BROCAK. Nothing happened. Stupid argument. *Forgotten.*

FRAU MERTEL So you say.

Enter WADEK KUZCIWSKI.

WADEK *has a take-away sausage.*

WADEK KUZCIWSKI (*to* MERTEL). Oh. Good afternoon. Not mad no more? No? You have to drink. To hold out. Yeah. Drink and sing. Not like this here. Real party. Like back home. Vodka and girls and then *dancing.* Aw shit, I've no luck with women. Eh? Anna. Have I luck?

FRAU MERTEL (*not knowing what to do*). Yeah er? It's alright.

WADEK KUZCIWSKI. We shake now hands. Yes? Friends.

FRAU MERTEL. Er yeah . . .

WADEK KUZCIWSKI. Er . . . Er . . . I'm only a stupid Pole.
I know. A Pollack. Poor and stupid. Always was in way of
ladies and gentlemen. But new Germany. Help us. Not so?
She like us more as others. All this riff raff. (*Laughs*.) Half
Poland is nearly German. We bit related. Bit.

FRAU MERTEL. You'd help yourselves. It will be better and
then you will also . . . (*Irritated*.) Oh what . . . That's idiotic
too.

WADEK KUZCIWSKI. You have to be a dog. You understand?
Then crawl out of yesterday. On all fours. It's impossible to
walk upright. Ten years ago. You understand. We tried it.
We shouted. *So-li-dar-nosz!* (*Laughs*.) But then quickly
again down on all fours. Grovel. Grovel. Best is. If I was to
lose my paws. Lay down on my gut. Because I want a very
small. Half chewed bone. From the German dog handlers.
Please. Throw good doggie a bone!

FRAU MERTEL. Dogs never interested me. I don't like
dogs. You see that's how it is. There are lots of reasons.
(MERTEL *offers* WADEK *her hand*.) So? Are we friends
again?

WADEK *stares but doesn't give her his hand.* MERTEL
pauses, turns away.

WADEK KUZCIWSKI. Did anyone seen TV? A hostel has
burnt. A baby has burnt.

ELENA MAILOVIC. They are all together against us.

ANNA BROCAK. Some want not. They speaking good.

LAJOS BROCAK. Yeah Anna. And rub onions in their eyes.
(*Laughs*.) For the camera.

WADEK KUZCIWSKI (*to* MERTEL). You not. Need
residency permit. Not citizenship. The immigration police
say. *Your lot have free-market now. Just like us.* (*Laughs*.)
No reason to beg here.

FRAU MERTEL (*to* MARIA). Where are the children?

MARIA BROCAK. Children good.

FRAU MERTEL. Yes. I know. But where *are* they?

LAJOS BROCAK. Jesus. They run all over like young horses. Don't want to sit with old people. Only Anna always there. You see? Anna's my gold.

WADEK KUZCIWSKI. Ha! The children. I can take you to the children. *Auntie Social.* Where are the little ones? Begging again at every house. What else? Bring everything to later Papa. They're also gold. Eh?

ANNA BROCAK. Why these lies? Why us? Always us? (*To* WADEK.) That cruel. What we wrong.

WADEK KUZCIWSKI. No. I . . . Excuse me, Anna. You I don't mean . . . You are . . . You . . .

ANNA BROCAK. You say bad my brother. My family.

WADEK KUZCIWSKI. He stole from me. Your father.

ANNA BROCAK. You are no better.

WADEK KUZCIWSKI. No? But there's a difference.

LAJOS BROCAK (*springs up*). You stop this sick. You little shit.

LAJOS *wants to attack* WADEK *but notices* MERTEL *and sits.*

LAJOS BROCAK. All crazy!

GALINA DUVIDOWITSCH. That's right. Fight each other. One against the other. Beat your heads bloody amongst yourselves. It's the neo-nazi's job. But you save them trouble. That very good. They happy! They don't have to start any more fires. Again they've time for dancing and enjoy themselves.

WADEK KUZCIWSKI. That they want to get rid of such sub-humans. They are right.

VEDRAN MAILOVIC. Because Pollacks is good friends with Germans.

VEDRAN *laughs.*

WADEK KUZCIWSKI. In Poland beat up a Gypo one time. They piss off. Peace.

ANNA BROCAK. Now you said it. You always smiling me. Say Anna come. Anna come sit.

WADEK KUZCIWSKI. I didn't mean it so. (*Disturbed.*) What you want?

ANNA BROCAK. Not so fun. I much fear. Always fear.

WADEK KUZCIWSKI. Is OK. I didn't want . . . I'm sorry Anna.

FRAU MERTEL. But Anna *not.* Not in *this* town. Here are just normal people. At worst they complain a little.

GALINA DUVIDOWITSCH. No really?

GALINA *points out into the yard where ASYLANTEN RAUS! can still be read.*

GALINA DUVIDOWITSCH (*as if she reads*). A-big-warm-wel-come! You see? (GALINA *points to* ANNA.) And she loves to go out in the streets. Because everyone is always so nice to her. No one wants to hurt her. They love that she's come to Germany and kiss her! A few people complain. But only because they're bored. Anna's had her warm welcome!

FRAU MERTEL. There's been isolated riots . . .

GALINA DUVIDOWITSCH. Riots! But not the funny kind of riot!

FRAU MERTEL. . . . . isolated attacks. But from totally disturbed people. Alcoholics. Unemployed. Youths. Half children. They're not nazis. And we shouldn't brand them that. It will only make them that really. We've to care more about them. Help them understand their lives. Give them a future.

ELENA MAILOVIC. Yes. Help. Because they are hungry. They are refugees from war. Them. Not us.

WADEK KUZCIWSKI. Whilst everyone is box-eyed with nazi terror no one sees the state slide more and more right!

MARIA BROCAK (*to* MERTEL). Frau. You not see? Bad everything. Bad. And no washing helps.

VEDRAN MAILOVIC. Nazi. Not nazi. All the same what you call them when they hit with steel pipe. Stab with knifes.

MARIA BROCAK. People all bad.

GALINA DUVIDOWITSCH. No. You have to give them money. Youth clubs. Teachers. Priests. Social workers. They must all speak to them nicely. The police too. They must help. Laugh. Caress. Not arrest them. Are they murderers? Or just dumb children playing some nonsense?

FRAU MERTEL. And how else should we solve the problem? Locking them up is no solution!

ELENA MAILOVIC. No. No solution? But locking up us is always solution.

LAJOS BROCAK. When I only ride on bus without pay, I get punished. Jail maybe? Deportation.

VEDRAN MAILOVIC. We also humans without protection. But these nazis have the right pass! You born here. You need never ask what you can do. Piss on the street. Or piss on me!

WADEK KUZCIWSKI. It's really a shame that people behave so badly. That they've so little understanding. I'm often insulted. I know how it is. The citizens' group that meets in the church hall. They are against this *Ausländerfiendlicheit*. This . . . hostility to foreigners. I know they get threatening letters and anonymous phone calls.

LAJOS BROCAK. No one will drive you away from here. You understand?

FRAU MERTEL. The people are only afraid. Afraid of the unknown. To lose their jobs. To lose law and order. Fear turns into this senseless racism.

LAJOS BROCAK. Racism only fever. But the sickness. That's the difference between the rich and the poor.

ELENA MAILOVIC. They not want give up from what they have enough.

FRAU MERTEL. We have to find understanding for each other. Come closer and dismantle the prejudice.

Enter PJOTR PAJEWSKI.

PJOTR PAJEWSKI *carries a book.*

WADEK KUZCIWSKI. The Professor. Good afternoon.

PJOTR PAJEWSKI. What? Oh you. I *said.* Let me in peace. Please. (*Absently into the room.*) My wife's not here? I can't find my shoes.

WADEK KUZCIWSKI. We should dismantle prejudice. (*Of* MERTEL.) She says so. (*To* PJOTR.) What have I done you?

PJOTR PAJEWSKI (*to* MERTEL). By the way. The washing machine has been broken for weeks. And the caretaker doesn't allow us to wash by hand in the shower or the kitchen.

They all stare at MERTEL. PJOTR *looks around bewildered. The stares move gradually to* PJOTR.

PJOTR PAJEWSKI. He's now drunk again. Singing the national anthem. And folk songs. However. The washing machine. He should . . . could he? . . . Yahh . . .

Exit PJOTR PAJEWSKI.

GALINA DUVIDOWITSCH (*to* MERTEL). You always take the trouble . . .

FRAU MERTEL. Me . . . Tonight we'll put everything else off until later. Sit together. And enjoy ourselves.

WADEK KUZCIWSKI (*whisper*). Anna.

FRAU MERTEL. I'm all excited about your different dishes. The *Pelmini.* Herr Brocak's lamb kebabs. When you've really for the first time got to know each other. And stick together. Everything will be easier. Who knows? Perhaps one day we can cook for visitors. Have a sort of open day. People from the town could talk with you. See how difficult life really is for you all.

LAJOS BROCAK. I not want know them. Not bring here.

FRAU MERTEL. Well. I've to be quick. I'm bringing home-made cheese pasta like they eat where I come from. See you later.

WADEK KUZCIWSKI (*whisper*). Yes. Fuck off. (*Louder.*) Just a joke. The children play in the park. I saw them earlier.

GALINA DUVIDOWITSCH. What's up with you? . . . You're trembling . . .

FRAU MERTEL. Oh a. No. I'm only nervous.

WADEK KUZCIWSKI (*apes* MERTEL). *Only ner-vous.* (*Laughs.*) Always nervous. When are you not ner-vous? If someone here has reason to be nervous then it's us. Me. (*Laughs.*) You have worries? Is Anna ner-vous?

FRAU MERTEL. In time . . . my work became my dream job because I really wanted. Wanted to help . . .

WADEK KUZCIWSKI. How touching but don't lie. No man wanted to throw a white veil over your head. That why! Help! (*Laughs.*) No I don't help.

FRAU MERTEL. I must go. We'll all see each other later. OK . . . er. See you later.

Exit FRAU MERTEL.

WADEK KUZCIWSKI (*to* VEDRAN). *Because I really wanted to help.* (*Laughs.*) She talk us bollocks. Moaning because no one else listens.

GALINA DUVIDOWITSCH. Now on we celebrate. Forget this pigsty. Laugh!

ANNA BROCAK (*to* WADEK). This pot is heavy. You help me carry to table?

LAJOS BROCAK. All crazy. At end we singing *together!?*

GALINA DUVIDOWITSCH. Why not? Why not?

WADEK KUZCIWSKI. Eat together . . . she only wants to watch us. She nice. Always nice. But who pays her? State.

ANNA BROCAK. Yeah yeah.

WADEK KUZCIWSKI. She work for state that only want quickly rid of us.

Blackout.

3

*Late Sunday evening. The kitchen's an orgy of colour, different
cuts and kinds of meat, vegetables and fruit.* ELENA *prepares
a party-style* Djuvec, LJUDMILA *a* Borschtsch. VEDRAN
Srpski Avjar, ANNA *and* MARIA *stuff vine leaves and*
GALINA *makes an Oriental-Jewish sweet mousse.* LAJOS
smokes and makes kebab skewers. MICHAIL *drinks vodka.*
PJOTR, *constantly in the way, has a book and a newspaper
with him but never really reads.*

MICHAIL DUVIDOWITSCH. *Nastrowje!* Drink. Drink. Then
everything tastes better.

GALINA DUVIDOWITSCH. Help Michail. Don't just get
drunk.

MICHAIL DUVIDOWITSCH. Let the Jew drink. Jew wants to
get pissed. Like a real Ukrainian! And no Jewish food you!
We want food like back home.

GALINA DUVIDOWITSCH. You are spoiling the good mood.

LJUDMILA PAJEWSKAJA. But please. We must have at least
one Jewish dish.

MICHAIL DUVIDOWITSCH. *Njet.* Kosher meat stinks! And
always meat and milk separate! No good sauce. Shit! Real
shit.

ANNA BROCAK. But you're Jewish yourself. How you can
complain?

MICHAIL DUVIDOWITSCH. Exactly. Exactly because I am.
It's terrible. Completely terrible. I don't like Jews.

ELENA MAILOVIC. You can't all the same . . . I mean . . .
Home I know very decent friendly family. The woman . . .

VEDRAN MAILOVIC. Elena! You know nothing about it.

MICHAIL DUVIDOWITSCH. Yes. Oh yes. Exactly that you can! They all same. All criminals. The Jews are to blame! Always. Yes! At home the communists Jews. Traitors to their country Jews. In America bankers millionaires Jews. And here? Jews Jews Jews. The poor Jews. Oh dear Hitler gassed them. But because of it they cram their shit up German arses!

GALINA DUVIDOWITSCH. What rubbish!

PJOTR PAJEWSKI (*cynical*). Why do you foul yourself? It's so overdone. This Jewish megalomania. You're not so important. And more so. Who really is interested? The whole of earth is suffocating. Dying. The environment my man. There's a real catastrophe. There are much more important problems than this eternal complex. Such nonsense about banks and America . . . Despair at nuclear dangers. At least that has a future. Or the ozone layer for example. Do you ever consider such subjects?

MICHAIL DUVIDOWITSCH (*points, desperate*). This. This too. Whose fault is the hole? All the Jew. All that smoke from Auschwitz's crematoriums. Too many Jews. Too much smoke. The hole!

PJOTR PAJEWSKI. Oh yeah . . .

ANNA BROCAK. You please. Not drink no more . . .

ELENA MAILOVIC. You have simple no reason . . .

VEDRAN MAILOVIC. Don't interfere. Leave it.

ELENA MAILOVIC. Good good.

LAJOS BROCAK. All crazy.

PJOTR PAJEWSKI. That's enough. This rubbish is obscene.

    Exit PJOTR PAJEWSKI.

LJUDMILA PAJEWSKAJA. There he goes. Uh oh . . .

GALINA DUVIDOWITSCH. He's a difficult person.

LJUDMILA PAJEWSKAJA. No he's only sensitive. You see. He can't stand shouting. Can't work can't think.

ELENA MAILOVIC. He not speak us and know better.

LJUDMILA PAJEWSKAJA. No one here knows but he was a clever professor. That's what makes him so . . . so funny.

LAJOS BROCAK. Why no children? Then must care children and not time to knot head.

LAJOS gestures, he's crazy.

LJUDMILA PAJEWSKAJA. That again? Children now? For what?

MICHAIL DUVIDOWITSCH. *Kinder?* Ask my wife. Have you a child? You not alone any more. Can kiss little idiot from head to toe. Sugar here sweetie there. Can tell it stories and cry and moan. Not need speak your husband more. He is only in the way. Child need love. Need kisses. Cover. (*Laughs.*) But when my son grow up. Then we go drink together with no Mama.

Enter WADEK KUZCIWSKI.

WADEK KUZCIWSKI. A surprise from me! Cake for everyone. (*To* LJUDMILA). Your husband's an idiot!

LJUDMILA PAJEWSKAJA (*to* ELENA). Taste? That is good *Borschtsch.* What a joy! A real *Borschtsch.* Red and thick!

MICHAIL DUVIDOWITSCH. He's a good boy. Not matter what she try do. Not talk with me. Not matter. I love my son!

WADEK KUZCIWSKI. Your husband's a loser!

LJUDMILA PAJEWSKAJA. What do you want?

WADEK KUZCIWSKI. Nothing, not a thing. Life's beautiful. Only he stays stupid. Don't know a good offer. Don't want earn Deutsch Mark. He is rather something special. I have friendly idea for him to make a bit of money. And what? He don't need friend? Say he don't listen. (*To* LAJOS.) Here hand cigarettes? Me not give shit! You good businessman. Clever like Wadek. Big clever. You Anna's Father we no

fight. Not angry more colleague? Her husband not like us.
For him we shit from bottom of tip.

LAJOS BROCAK. Me not angry. Have forgotten.

WADEK KUZCIWSKI. I like your daughter. Anna come here.

LAJOS *gestures to* ANNA, *'keep away'.*

LAJOS BROCAK. Me too. You understanding?

WADEK KUZCIWSKI (*sits*). Yes but yes I.

MICHAIL DUVIDOWITSCH. Do you want to drink, Pole?

WADEK KUZCIWSKI. *Nastrowje.*

GALINA DUVIDOWITSCH. Oh very sweet?

ANNA BROCAK. What from it made?

GALINA DUVIDOWITSCH. Oh. So simple. Only apples
nuts grated almonds. Stirred with cinnamon and white wine.
A small spoon of sugar. Ready!

MICHAIL DUVIDOWITSCH. Vodka! Vodka tastes better.
(*Laughs.*) Shalom!

ANNA BROCAK. Yes. Sweet is good after savoury. The
mutton pilao is spicy. Mamma wraps it in vine. And put
back in frying pan!

MICHAIL DUVIDOWITSCH. The whole house with garlic
stinked.

WADEK KUZCIWSKI. You know this one? Romanian move
out tomorrow. But stink? Not for another ten years.

MICHAIL DUVIDOWITSCH. I don't care. Rather
Romanian . . .

WADEK KUZCIWSKI. What?

MICHAIL DUVIDOWITSCH. Rather Romanian than Jew.

WADEK KUZCIWSKI (*laughs*). Ah!

ANNA BROCAK. At last come cream on top.

MICHAIL DUVIDOWITSCH (*laughs*). That won't help!
(*To* WADEK.) *Nastrowje.*

LAJOS BROCAK. You can stuff your face with German mush
from Social Lady. (*Laughs.*) No garlic there and nothing
special too.

ELENA MAILOVIC (*uncertain*). In my *Djuvec* also garlic.
But no mutton. Only pork. Lamb. Beef neck. Onions.
Peppers. Beans. Tomatoes. All boil until it thick.

WADEK KUZCIWSKI. Good. It almost like *Bigosz.*

ELENA MAILOVIC. Ah . . . is there parsley left?

WADEK KUZCIWSKI. In *Bigosz* is mushrooms. Got to be!

GALINA DUVIDOWITSCH. Aha!

MICHAIL DUVIDOWITSCH (*to* GALINA). But the boy not
eat any mushrooms. You hear me? No mushrooms! Who
can say if they are poisonous.

VEDRAN MAILOVIC. Anyone have complaints about my
Avjar?

ANNA BROCAK (*laughs*).What in? What in?

VEDRAN MAILOVIC. A pasta starter with aubergines and
peppers. And er. You have from excuse me. Garlic too!

GALINA DUVIDOWITSCH. Just not put plate near pot from
your wife. Or straightaway is tribal war again.

ELENA MAILOVIC. And with you is all peaceful. What?

LJUDMILA PAJEWSKAJA. Everything about ready. Now all
that missing is my husband and Frau Social Worker. Then
we may start our fight over forks!

VEDRAN MAILOVIC. When it possible for your husband. To
sit at same table as us.

LJUDMILA PAJEWSKAJA. What's wrong with you? He
wouldn't hurt a fly!

WADEK KUZCIWSKI. He comes. He eat even so. His sort
can takes as long as keeps clean hands. Main thing keep

clean hands! He fearing his own reflection because it could be show somewhere a small mark!

LJUDMILA PAJEWSKAJA. That's how his laws are. Decency. Honesty . . . and always polite.

WADEK KUZCIWSKI (*laughs*). Right now fantastically polite. (*Cruelly.*) He's a hypocrite that's all. Anyway what we wait? Auntie Social not come. Old goat have second thoughts. (*Laughs.*) Can she really lick clean the bowl with the likes of us?

ELENA MAILOVIC. It stinks again! It makes me really sick.

WADEK KUZCIWSKI. That's what she should care about. To at last get knackered drains fixed. The blocked bog. Or tell us why for hours the heating not work. She definitely not come.

GALINA DUVIDOWITSCH. Nonsense. It was her idea.

ANNA BROCAK. Wadek come. Sit! Are you sad?

LAJOS BROCAK. Reasonable plan. Eat together then easier live together. There is old words. *One plate one heart.*

WADEK KUZCIWSKI. All hypocrites.

ANNA BROCAK. No more. Today you dance with me. Today yes. Father let us. It party. No bad words. Promise!

WADEK KUZCIWSKI. But she not *have* to live here. Not share this shit. Police searches. Why should she eat with us.

MARIA BROCAK. Rubbish! What you looking? The woman is good!

LAJOS BROCAK. We wait.

WADEK KUZCIWSKI. Wait anyway for nothing. You understand me Anna?

ANNA BROCAK. Be quiet. (*Stares at* LAJOS. *No reaction.*) You important. Yes Wadek. Yes? Could be me too? Flowers . . . in my room. From you? Thank you!

WADEK KUZCIWSKI. You not notice her disgust? I know you notice.

ANNA BROCAK. Is not important.

LJUDMILA PAJEWSKAJA. The woman only want make better what is happening us in her country. Because she friendly.

ANNA BROCAK. She brings food! Say so.

WADEK KUZCIWSKI. Waiting? She definitely won't come. She's had enough! (*Laughs.*) Don't be angry Anna. I say nothing. Nothing more. (*Tender.*) As you are . . .

Enter PJOTR PAJEWSKI.

PJOTR *carries the corpse of* MERTEL. *The clothes torn like she was raped.*

PJOTR PAJEWSKI. I was out in the park. It is dark.

All stare at PJOTR *except* MICHAIL. *He drinks.*

PJOTR PAJEWSKI. For a walk. One is allowed to go for a walk!?

LAJOS BROCAK. What?

PJOTR PAJEWSKI. A mild night. A few stars . . . But everyone is busy.

MICHAIL DUVIDOWITSCH (*drunk, loud.*) Yes busy and very! What is wrong? (*Sees the corpse.*) Galina. We must go.

LAJOS BROCAK. What?

PJOTR PAJEWSKI. I said. It's dark pitch dark . . . but I found her anyway.

LJUDMILA PAJEWSKAJA. What?

PJOTR PAJEWSKI (*screams*). I don't know what! I don't know . . . Suddenly she is there laid next to the tulips. You will have seen them. Honestly I hate tulips. And really one should touch nothing. I know but . . . she couldn't *just* lie there.

PJOTR *lays* MERTEL's *corpse on the floor. He stands, shrugs helplessly. Everyone is silent.*

ANNA BROCAK (*slowly. half-conscious, to* WADEK). She-not-come.

WADEK KUZCIWSKI. Yeah . . .? What . . .? No!

LJUDMILA PAJEWSKAJA. Oh God!

ANNA *points at* WADEK, *her mouth open to scream, but no sound escapes . . .*

MARIA BROCAK (*horrified*). Anna!

Blackout.

4

Monday morning. Yesterday's food an the table, untouched.

LJUDMILA *butters bread: then circles the table, surveys the food.*

Enter PJOTR PAJEWSKI.

PJOTR PAJEWSKI. Is there any tea? (LJUDMILA *silent, stares at him.*) No jam for me Mila. This food stinks. Like some essence of the Balkans and death.

LJUDMILA PAJEWSKAJA. Eat! Eat everything up and enjoy it. Today at last you have your beloved peace. He not here anymore. Can't disturb you. Talking no more. Did you go to the Police?

PJOTR PAJEWSKI. As you know. No. I didn't. And anyway. What do you mean. *Talking no more?*

LJUDMILA PAJEWSKAJA. You know what I mean. You know very well.

PJOTR PAJEWSKI. What! Tomorrow he'll be back. And you can have him as your best friend.

LJUDMILA PAJEWSKAJA. When they believe he's a murderer . . . when it is different . . . he not come. Must stay. And is no evidence of other suspects . . . even though there is. Could be there is. Could be in your hand.

PJOTR PAJEWSKI. If he didn't do it. Tomorrow he'll be sitting back there grinning. The Police aren't stupid. And if he isn't released then good. I'll hand over the note. If it helps . . . I don't think so. It only gets in our way.

LJUDMILA PAJEWSKAJA. Of course you hand it over. How? What will you say? Explain it?

PJOTR PAJEWSKI. Yes . . . I have . . . forgot. Simply forgot it.
Tiredness. Yesterday's shock. I didn't realise that the note
was important. Only nonsense . . . It's possible.

LJUDMILA PAJEWSKAJA. They should punish you. Really.
How can anyone think that? Unbelievable. Someone is
taken by the Police and you don't care. There is a note.
You put it away. And watch. Watch an injustice. Maybe
an innocent man. And you don't care.

PJOTR PAJEWSKI. Innocent? He's not innocent. Never was!
This Pole has earned at least ten years in jail. How have
I damaged him? What damage? How can anyone stand it?
Always his shadow, Those dirty hands. His face . . .
Everywhere I turn. He always stand there. Why can him
not leave me alone? Why does he worm in my thought.
Whispering always. *You're no longer a Geologist! The Herr
Dr Pajewski! And you never will be again! You are just like
me. Look at me your mirror. Just like me!* I hate him! Yes
I fear him. And I'm not to blame Mila. I can't do anything
about it. He wanted it that way! I can't bear him. I am not
his friend. He'll help himself. His sort always do.

LJUDMILA PAJEWSKAJA. You know everything. Do everything right. True?

PJOTR PAJEWSKI. He's not worth it. Would he help us? Get
himself involved? He would do worse at any time.

LJUDMILA PAJEWSKAJA. Who knows. But it gives you no
right. The note you found is evidence. Maybe someone does
more murders because you don't help. Help? It's duty.

PJOTR PAJEWSKI (*from his shirt pocket*). It has no address
Mila. (*The note.*) Look. It's anonymous. The letters are cut
from a newspaper. Totally useless.

LJUDMILA PAJEWSKAJA. You must hand it in.

PJOTR PAJEWSKI. When . . . when I post it . . . without my
name . . .

LJUDMILA PAJEWSKAJA. Give me. (LJUDMILA *reads*.)
THE AS-YL-UM SL-AG GETS THIS. AND ALL OTH-ER RED CU-NTS.
GERMAN-Y FOR THE GER-MANS. SIEG HEIL! . . . That's vile filth.

PJOTR PAJEWSKI. If he wrote it himself. Listen . . .

LJUDMILA PAJEWSKAJA. Rubbish. He was *here!* When should he have killed her? When!?

PJOTR PAJEWSKI. He was away for a while. To kill someone Mila. That's quickly done. Very quickly. I want to know nothing. Nothing. And anyone could have done this note. Any one of us. Or anyone else.

LJUDMILA PAJEWSKAJA. You want to know anything. Bravo! That is why we left. Come here. So that it all come with us. Sticks in our backs. Clings to our clothes. Our skin. Fear. Cruelty. Lies and nothing. Always know nothing. That why? Did we only want another country? Didn't we want to live different. Grow different. Be different.

PJOTR PAJEWSKI. What?

LJUDMILA PAJEWSKAJA. Human!

PJOTR PAJEWSKIJ. What . . . Don't confuse it all Mila . . . Yes. Of course but how . . . No. It's like this. The note was put under a stone. On the washroom windowsill. Coincidence that I . . . I found it. I mean. Not a comfortable position. Who put it there? Who wrote it? Why must I find it? It's dangerous. Very dangerous.

LJUDMILA PAJEWSKAJA. Why. Everything is so simple. (*Suddenly laughs.*) Or did you kill him?

PJOTR PAJEWSKI. What for?

LJUDMILA PAJEWSKAJA. Ach! You have no heart.

PJOTR PAJEWSKI. She lay like in a film. I understood nothing. Among the flowers the woman. She was dead. *Completely dead.* I knew that on the stairs . . . Her body was heavy.

LJUDMILA PAJEWSKAJA. Without the note and even so heavy . . .

PJOTR PAJEWSKI. What? Yes . . .

LJUDMILA PAJEWSKAJA. She need revenge!! One must punish. Find. Was she so unimportant in your world?

PJOTR PAJEWSKI. No. No. No man is unimportant. I know.
I was afraid! Worse. Fear of fear. And him. What did I think
of him? He drove a *car!* You understand? This country pays
for his living. And he drives around in a car! What should
people think?

LJUDMILA PAJEWSKAJA. He had a car? So what! How
many Poles did they kill in their concentration camps? So
he creams off a little from their good life. Well done! Why
are they are rich and we are not when *they* lost the war? If
he cheats . . . Who here has the right to judge him? Them!?
And why suddenly do you hide such important evidence?

PJOTR PAJEWSKI. Important what? That's fifty years ago!
Germany's a democratic state.

LJUDMILA PAJEWSKAJA. Yes? They are monsters from a
dark past. Full of hate. Inherited indestructible hate. They
want no witnesses in their landscape. Don't you get this?
Democracy!? It's cold here!

PJOTR PAJEWSKI. Now you're nervous Mila. I'll try to find a
way to hand over this bloody letter to the police. Without
making them suspicious of us.

LJUDMILA PAJEWSKAJA. Us?

PJOTR PAJEWSKI. I'm going now. Don't be stupid. Get
some rest.

Exit PJOTR PAJEWSKI.

LJUDMILA *sits and stares at her tea cup. Before she
speaks again it's as if her spirit has departed her.*

Enter VEDRAN.

VEDRAN MAILOVIC. That is all that is all . . . Good
morning . . . No one understands . . . What is the question?
(*Of the food.*) A funeral feast but no one eats. My wife is
asleep. This sort of thing is not good for the child. Whole
night just Police. Questions. Questions. Questions. What
can we know. Whom will be accused? Tell us! Quick!
(*To* LJUDMILA.) You is all white.

Enter LAJOS.

LAJOS BROCAK. Many dishes all full. Food enough for an army. But will we ever be full? Everyone's gone crazy! You can only laugh . . . Do you think he . . .

VEDRAN MAILOVIC. It looks so.

LAJOS BROCAK. Lot look so . . . as if it's. Do we know?

VEDRAN MAILOVIC. No. But who . . .?

LAJOS BROCAK. Yes. Who? A good question. Who? Is there only our hostel?

Enter GALINA *and* MICHAIL.

MICHAIL DUVIDOWITSCH. I believe. I have drank with him. Drank much. Much vodka. Now they ask questions. I don't answer. What should I think? I know no one here.

GALINA DUVIDOWITSCH. Evening meal together . . . and what must happen? *You have to understand me Frau Duvidowitsch.* That's what she said.

MICHAIL DUVIDOWITSCH. There is no reason. In the end there is no reason.

LAJOS BROCAK. Exactly.

VEDRAN MAILOVIC. What do you mean? Exactly?

LAJOS BROCAK. There is no reason. No one can grip it. Exactly that make it so bad.

LJUDMILA PAJEWSKAJA. Ah ha!

Enter MARIA.

MARIA BROCAK (*cries*). Poor woman poor poor woman. What a disaster. We are all black. Godless. In sleep I see black water. See black slime. Poor poor woman.

GALINA DUVIDOWITSCH. It's good. Come here. Calm yourself first.

MARIA BROCAK. No. That is blood. Blood must shout. Where is Anna? Poor woman. *Ai ai. Oh.* Poor poor woman.

GALINA DUVIDOWITSCH (*helpless*). But . . .

LAJOS BROCAK. Let it be. It's important. Only Maria. Only my wife knows the secret of grief. But us . . . I don't know . . .

GALINA DUVIDOWITSCH. We think of us. Of ourselves. Like everyone.

VEDRAN MAILOVIC. Yes. Yes. Exactly.

LAJOS BROCAK. What mean with *exactly?*

MARIA BROCAK. From murder we fled and now . . . Death laughs. Here behind these windows. I hear my mother my father whispering. I whisper too. With myself. *I am here father. Here. Come get me. Get me to you.* Lajos. Look. Everything is light. But I recognise nothing. Ai ai. The poor woman. What is to happen.

MARIA *sits at the table and buries her head in her arms.*

MICHAIL DUVIDOWITSCH. What's wrong with her?

GALINA DUVIDOWITSCH. Shush! You idiot!

Enter ELENA.

VEDRAN MAILOVIC. You not sleep?

ELENA MAILOVIC. Ach.

GALINA DUVIDOWITSCH. There we are and wait for nothing.

ELENA MAILOVIC. That we always do. Wait. Wait. A woman is murdered. No one has sympathy.

MICHAIL DUVIDOWITSCH. But. You can't simply say that . . .

ELENA MAILOVIC. I have no sympathy! Every night asleep at my feet I see dead children. Little children. Shot in head. White faced. Who allows them run to here? No one! Door shut! Sent back! Back to nightmare place. Ripped out arms in a soup from blood. I don't have left any sympathy.

VEDRAN MAILOVIC. Stop it come. Don't cry.

ELENA MAILOVIC (*quiet*). Police believe we all guilty. Test us like criminals. Not believe. (*To* LAJOS.) Brocak. They hear your daughter again. At the caretaker's.

LAJOS BROCAK. What!? Enough now! What shall she *speak?* The child have nothing to do with it!

Exit LAJOS *dragging* MARIA *with him.*

Exit all others except LJUDMILA.

LJUDMILA PAJEWSKAJA. One must get something . . . This note and me . . . It's all knotted . . . But me . . . Pjotr! Pjotr help! I silence. I silence too.

Enter PJOTR.

PJOTR PAJEWSKI. Mila! Mila!. Imagine this I . . .

Dumb, PJOTR *stares at* LJUDMILA.

LJUDMILA PAJEWSKAJA (*absently*). Yeah?

PJOTR PAJEWSKI (*kisses* LJUDMILA*'s forehead*). Imagine I have a letter . . .

LJUDMILA PAJEWSKAJA. What!?

PJOTR PAJEWSKI. *Not!* Quiet. *Listen.* We'll move out of here. We will stay.

LJUDMILA PAJEWSKAJA. What? Move out and stay?

PJOTR PAJEWSKI. Stay in Germany. Move out of here. Away. Away a way away! No longer strangers. I will be made a citizenship. I will be given a German passport.

LJUDMILA *stares horrified at* PJOTR.

Enter ANNA BROCAK.

ANNA BROCAK (*at the door*). All gone.

ANNA *wants to leave but stays, begins to cry, turns one more time.*

ANNA BROCAK. He is dead. Hanged. I . . . I believed . . . I believe maybe he it did . . . but I am blame.

LJUDMILA PAJEWSKAJA. The Pole?

PJOTR PAJEWSKI. He hanged himself?

ANNA BROCAK. I have not say. He himself have . . . himself hanged. Only hanged. In his cell.

Silence.

ANNA BROCAK. Nobody know. How alone he . . . I . . .

Exit ANNA BROCAK.

LJUDMILA PAJEWSKAJA. Congratulations.

PJOTR PAJEWSKI. Mila . . . It is not anything to do with me . . . It . . . would . . . anyway . . . Mila. Don't look at me like that. Always he threw his dirt at me. Even now . . . Oh God! He is dead.

LJUDMILA PAJEWSKAJA. Hand over note at the last. Now.

PJOTR PAJEWSKI. Whom could that help? Not *him*. Oh God. It's too late. Why could he not wait? Now. When all is good for us . . . All the trouble imagine it. No. They may put everything back. Reconsider. I would be a liar and then.

LJUDMILA PAJEWSKAJA. Then I will go. I tell it. It has to be known. If he did not do it!

PJOTR PAJEWSKI. Listen. It's too late! It's happened. Sadly. But it's happened. I will be ashamed Mila. Very ashamed. And put it right again. But here look. Here is the paper stamp and signature. Everything as it must be. I'll be German.

LJUDMILA PAJEWSKAJA. For sure! The entrance money you've paid.

PJOTR PAJEWSKI. Why torture me. I cannot. Our first goal . . . We have reached. Will you now destroy all that?

LJUDMILA PAJEWSKAJA. OK. Let's have a drink.

PJOTR PAJEWSKI. What do you want? What will you do?

LJUDMILA PAJEWSKAJA. Nothing. I am your wife. I will have a passport too.

PJOTR PAJEWSKI. And not tell about the note?

LJUDMILA PAJEWSKAJA. No. You burn it. Yes . . . No Pjotr.
It is good. We want a better life.

WADEK – *noose mark on his neck, his tongue dangling
from his mouth – and* MERTEL – *covered in bruises and
wounds, her teeth knocked out – dance like bride and groom
over the stage. The hostel dwellers, with the exception of the*
PAJEWSKIS, *come to the pair and throw confetti on them.
Suddenly they are black, brown, slant-eyed.*

Blackout.

JENNIFER KLEMM

OR

COMFORT AND MISERY OF THE LAST GERMANS

Ten sentences from German contemporary life
with

NOTES FOR THE STAGE

by D. Rust

translated by Rosee Riggs

D. Rust was born in 1959 in East Berlin and grew up between Berlin and Brandenburg. She has been writing drama, poems and essays for 14 years and *Jennifer Klemm oder Trost und Elend der letzten Deutschen*, her second play, was first performed in Hannover in June, 1995. Her other work includes *Der Flop*, *Das Trio*, and *Lachmanns Villa*. D. Rust lives in Stahnsdorf near Potsdam.

Jennifer Klemm or Comfort and Misery of the Last Germans was first performed in English as part of the *New German Voices* season in the Theatre Upstairs on 6 October 1995 with the following cast:

Maureen Beattie
Gary Curran
Ian Hughes
Jack James
Dorit Rust
Andy Serkis

Translator and Director   Rosee Riggs

to the Milliner, to the Beauty,
to the Good-for-nothing, to the
laughing Third Party

I

Germancountry Music

Lights up on stage. A chair in shadow, centre. Three or any number of harvest festival wreaths are moved slowly up and down. A young intellectual in a flowing coat comes on. He has brought a tuba; occupies the chair. While he speaks, he begins to sway from side to side. Increasingly strongly.

THE INTELLECTUAL. **Germancountry Music**
Ooohhowpleaeaeasant lihiife is getting drunk doesn't cost
the earthearthearth like edelweiß And the folk yesthefolk
yesthefolkyesthefolkfolkfolk they just like living because
dying takes doughdough doesn't it and beyond ones means one
just cannot Can one one
doesn't have to be wealthywealthy to be
wealthywealthy A bit of peaeace
Gimmegimmegimme abitofpeace
A bit of peace does help us along though The wars are of course
more numerous but then they are smaller Also they don't
last so terribly long any more Theydon't lastlonganymore
lastlonganymore
January to March is quite sufficient for suchua-tio-ua-
tioua tioua incidents
After all summer is the high season and
who doesn't need sunshine
shinealittleshine
at least on holiday
Holladihihaholladihoholadihihaholadi –
My name is Jennifer Klemm and hello to daddy and to
Herr Bundeskanzler And all together now: That's-why-it-is-
so fine-on-Rhine . . .

II

Subsidising Films

Youths, meaningless, superfluous. The stage is a wall with the advertisement of a bank on it. Someone speaks the text: anyone.

Eh Guv you coming along Where's it on In the 'World' What's on there? 'Fucking World' Are you coming No man It's too expensive in the 'World' My old man's out of work Watch 'Fucking World' without a ticket man Man no way you're seen once in the world you're on the list Twice the pigs are there Third time you're in the nick Like my old man landed up No thanks the nick no Nothing but shit then shit you only live once: Frightened of the pigs I do not believe it Go fuck yourself arsehole.

Blackout.

III

Müller's Office

MÜLLER *at desk.* KLEMM *runs busily backwards and forwards, basically rather distraught. Continually carrying files.*

MÜLLER. A mess again the like of which has never been there we must put the files in order in the files the ten poems against above all the state datedatedate *rubber stamps* date – ten Who knows how one can prove one's convictions later **oh well** An essay lovely very lovely not half oh well An anthem – tsch we get all Wastepaper basket No – you never know – Out again *out of the wastepaper basket* Archives! *rubber stamps* Strictly confidential *rubber stamps* Remember where! *writes, then to Klemm:* Don't worry Frau Klemm, a few more days . . . and you do get overtime too . . .

KLEMM. All the past into the cellarthedustbinintotheshredder! Not that it was good – or was it? It was sometimes good too. Anyway not so bad . . . Well sometimes – Still . . . all that work all those years . . .

MÜLLER. Her always conjuring up the past. You don't get far with an attitude like that. Any further. Certainly not. It just hinders what it's *tips out a filing drawer* actually about . . . Constantly looking to the past hinders a better future. Frau Klemm: E s s e n t i a l. Do look forward!

KLEMM. If I shouldn't look back, then how do I know if the future's better? I mean b e t t e r relates to something . . .

MÜLLER *gets a lipstick out of a drawer, pauses a moment.* Jen – You drive one mad with your questions. How do I know – Future is future. Just always better. Always! Because it brings hope. New hope. If a person knows life's going to go on, then How is a lower priority . . . I mean we no longer

knew how it would go on . . . Did we? *continues to himself*
Letter to father Intimate Very intimate   Under M   M for
misunderstanding Eleventwelvethirteen *turning pages* –
twenty petitions against contamination: of the ground by
sewage of sewage by pollutants of children's heads by lice of
children'sheadsbyprejudiceofprejudicebyweaponsofourown
weaponsbyharmlessnessofharmlessnessbystupidity . . . of
stupidity by violence V   V   Vi   Violence *filing card box*
Further to the files: t.t.f.   t.t.f. *rubber stamps*   These
towersofstrengththesetowersofpeoplethesetowersofthestate   i
jayjay *rummages among files* kkk   k   *upstage:* Where is the
L file?

KLEMM *from upstage.* For love?

MÜLLER. For 'Ludwig', Frau Klemm, for Ludwig *wiping last
crumbs from the table* Now there is order here again and
rising, to KLEMM   whatever else is to do we'll drop under
the table   *does up the top button on her blouse* and we'll drop
the pleasantries   *pressing* KLEMM *on to her   chair and
demonstrating to her mental eye with a motion of his hand:*
The nameplate: Bureau Müller – Limited Company   . . .
then looking at her and trying to be comforting· Unlimited
vistas . . . Company, Frau Klemm . . . Vistas –

IV

The One Year Nine to Twelve

The set is in darkness, a room on a podium. An actress enters the stage.

ACTRESS. He told me to do him an old woman. An old woman
like old women are . . . old woman . . . Me . . . an **old woman**
. . . Of course he means one like I think he imagines an old
woman must be nowadays. At my age! . . . Alright. Let him
have her. He doesn't just want to see the old woman. No . . .
nono. His own imagination is enough for that. He wants to
see **my** old woman. He wants to take m e apart, he wants to
display my view of an old woman . . . But I shall display his
for him . . . *upstage* HIS! He'll think I'm stupid. Incapable
of critical thought. Too much feeling. Too much empathy . . .
STRAIGHT FROM THE GUTS !! He can't bear it when he
can't think that I'm stupid. That I have too much empathy; he
hates it if he can't reproach me with my guts . . . There are
only two variations, TWO: I play him **his** old woman and free
myself from him . . . from this dictation, this . . . or I play him
mine *theatrically* m i n e, which he can kill! me with. *Pause*
Perhaps I'll do a bit of both, *laconically* he would have deserved
it. He would have deserved that. Without a doubt. But the
theme – all the same, it is . . . it is interesting. Significant.
One could almost say of *hesitatingly* . . . general interest . . .

The actress walks on to the set. Switches on the light.
Nightdress, makes up, switches off the light, gets into bed
in the dark. Morning from off: lights up slowly, street.
The room with the coffee-machine etc; all very cramped.
The radio alarm clock plays Cat Stevens' 'Morning has
broken . . . '. A slapping noise from the back.

THE OLD WOMAN. R e v o l t i n g. Simply revolting. Filthy
creatures. Go for the leftovers. These filthy creatures. No one

can devour so much bread. Where does the old cow get so much leftover bread . . . *very loudly over her head* No one can devour so much bread, n o o n e! . . . if I catch her once more – my God is that revolting . . . *'like the first bird . . . ', imitating the neighbour:* . . . the poor animals . . . They are filthy. Filthy! This dirt. This disgusting dirt. Dis-gus-ting. It's already sticking their wings together, it's sticking them up. And they shit . . . , shit up all my windows . . . *louder:* ' . . . *praise for them singing, praise for the morning . . . '.*

The old woman stands up, leaves the set. Upstage. Toilet flushes. Comes back; hair done, dressed, the top layer is an apron overall. Tears a page from the calendar, looks for her glasses, reads silently, adjusts radio.

THE OLD WOMAN. Can't even sing German any more . . . *turns knob . . .* **nowhere** *– turns off the radio. Tidies her hair again, lays the table for one person. Conscientiously. Sits down. Waits. Silence, till the coffee machine has switched itself off.*

ACTRESS *into OFF.* God almighty, I can't have breakfast for ever! We're not making a film here! *The old woman off the set. Toilet flushes. Re-enters. Another page off the calendar. Reads, TV on; different programmes: stock exchange, porno films, cartoons . . . TV off again. She makes the bed, sits down, stares at the telephone. Waits. Leaves the set.*

THE OLD WOMAN. I thought . . . Sorry. I thought it was for me . . . Also might not have been there. I would have taken the telegram for you. I wouldn't have minded. Really. Sorry. It is quite normal . . . am- . . . *door bangs* -ong neighbours . . . *enters the set. Sits at the table, stares at the telephone. Waits. Puts the telephone on the table. Waits. Suddenly picks up the receiver. At first soundlessly, then getting into the role of a conversation.*

THE OLD WOMAN. Yes. My name is Klemm. Oh it's you. Listen, so soon. You shouldn't, it costs so much, you have to watch it too . . . But I'm pleased. Of course I'm pleased. Yes, alright. No, better. It's better now. And you? What did you say? And the children? What did you say? Oh that's nice. I don't know. I don't know if I've got time. One is so busy. You don't understand, you young people. But you're always busy as well . . . continually. Of course I'm pleased. And how. But we don't want to talk too long. If someone rings now, someone can be ringing now . . . the phone is engaged again for so long . . . Well why shouldn't anyone ring? Alright. The weekend after next. Yes, wait a moment . . . I'll just go and look. Hold on, you . . . oh, and the little one? . . . Yesyes, I'll be quick, just wait a mo *goes to the calendar, takes off a new page, back to the telephone* . . . yes, today's the seventeenth already! Hey, listen what's written here on this here . . . 'the smile that you radiate will not return to you chinese proverb' . . . Oh will return . . . Oh it will return will it? Yes: will return to you . . . Alright. The weekend after next. Yes alright, I am pleased, of course. But I must go now. Can you hear me? And many thanks. Can you hear me? Yes. To all of you too. And to you. And to them . . . *puts phone down* . . . Bye . . . *pause* Lots of love . . . *pause. The old woman puts the telephone back. Waits. Crumples up the page from the calendar, puts it in her apron pocket. Waits. Gets the page out, smooths it out. All very carefully.*

THE OLD WOMAN. They always have nice sayings . . . Really. Nice sayings . . . *puts it in a drawer* . . .

The actress leaves the set, puts on lipstick, loosens her hair. Satisfied. Goes off quickly.

On the set the telephone rings.

V

Laughing about the Day Before the Day After

Middle-aged married couple. The man alone in the light. Reading the newspaper. In the dark next to him the woman, continually rubbing her hands on a cloth, not moving from the spot.

MAN *holding back from bursting out laughing all the time.* . . . in the desert you'll kill yourself laughing **YOU!** Come here Come over here a moment you really must Oh come on *wants to explode with laughter* **Madam Clamped!** Now will you come over here the silly buggers God are they silly . . .

MAN'S WIFE *after bowing to the audience and concentrating with an effort but without moving out of the shadow.* Yes, what is it then, what's the matter?

MAN. It's reported here in the paper alright get this it's written here: tatatata tatatata . . . more . . . tata – here: that American soldiers in the desert in Iraq are pushing up *renewed attack of laughing* are pushing up – sorry – the daisies.

MAN'S WIFE *absently.* Yes so Well there is one of one of those wars now.

MAN. Yes, don't you understand Don't you understand? In the desert! **D E S E R T!** Can you push up daisies in a desert then . . . *grins* God these silly buggers God

MAN'S WIFE. But if they're dead That's really sad That's really terrible Simply terrible Bound to be very young lads Very young *soundless* Isn't there anything written about it?

MAN. Don't you understand the joke, no you don't understand it **DEE EE ES AR TEE** – desert! You're talking about the lads I'm talking about the words here . . . It is actually terrible

it is If I counted up the dead in the newspaper every day, I'd
never get around finding everything terrible never get around
I'm talking about the words About the words You can't
understand the world any more these days any way **I** hold on
to the words They are a joke Or *getting increasingly excited*
Is that too high for your thick skull eh? Any joke and you can
ruin it with your dimwittedness your I didn't have to call you
you know I might have known you wouldn't understand it
You never understood a joke Never Just humourless Spend
the whole day doing nothing but cleaning What else can a
humourless person Nothing but c l e a n i n g and walking
around You got nothing to complain about Absolutely
nothing to complain about *to himself* But it's really good:
struggling to laugh as heartily as before pushing up the
daisies . . . in the desert.

The woman in the light. The man in the dark, motionless.

MAN'S WIFE. Humourless My father always used to say that
too He always said child, you don't understand a joke At
every opportunity when there was something to laugh about
And it was funny sometimes I did think it was funny
sometimes But I didn't dare laugh: They would have thought
I was laughing about them after all Then there would have
been trouble there would Father for example Once he nearly
exploded with laughter: **Girl** And he couldn't contain
himself Tears! he laughed: You have absolutely no wit *coy,
boyish* And the best thing is *shrieks with laughter –
containing herself again:* I haven't either.

210

VI

Canon

A group of five people, men and woman, at a table. In the background a saxophone player. All speak the same text, staggering the cues. They repeat this several times; interrupted by sudden light changes on to the saxophone player who has a short solo while the group at the table suspend speech and movement. At the next light change, the group simply continues with their words and behaviour as though they had never been interrupted. The length of time between the arbitrary interruptions becomes shorter and shorter as does the duration of the saxophone solos. At some place in the script the end is indicated by the last light change. The saxophonist with a high shrill note. Lights out.

‖: imagine I am of the opinion I am not of the opinion   that is my opinion do you want to know my opinion if you want to know my opinion if you ask me I tell you if I might just say something you cannot imagine it   I can't imagine that butbutbut   I wonder what makes you think that   why do you think that   well come now   that's just it!   I ask you what makes you think that imagine thinking that butbutbutbut now you're talking your way out of it *laughter* nononono you may take my word for it   you can take my word for it   you must take my word for it   I contradict categorically ohyesohyesohyes   should I take your word on that   but I must contradict you there   quite categorically contradict   he said   please   let me finish what I'm saying look I really must ask you   let me finish what I'm saying for once he said   she said they said   we said   they said I said :‖

VII

Tabloid Illusion

Imprisoned in a small space. Silence.

MAN. She had said what I should do then And that irritability
She was always irritable now So terribly irritable Any little
thing which one . . . Take your hands off Cynical! She had
become cynical **Is it any wonder when someone is always
so cynical!** Sure she said A child Bang the old lady to keep
her busy God! I don't want any more children Don't you
understand that Kathleen is sixteen do you see sixteen –
When I hold a baby in my arms I don't feel anything anymore
Do you see: nothing Can't you understand that A child isn't
work It's the norm the norm As long as you're young or
everything's fine or you're madly in love and as soon as one
of these – just one – is not the case nothing is normal any more
But I want to be normal do you hear – she said Quite normal
like . . . Take your paws off Quietly Quite quietly So –
sadly I hardly dared any more . . . not even stroke her hair . . .
And if you do work at the Post Office I said delivering mail
If you do Frau Wagner has it good Sure Quite quietly: sure
I can great And there's money too I don't need to ask you –
she said Don't need to ask you if you'll give me money for
your favourite perfume Afterallit'sforyou don't need to say
anything Sure It's no problem for me Not a bit: no
Müllermeierschulze – unfortunately – nothing today a few
invitations to bus trips in the immediate something about that
too nothing else unfortunately . . . And then she screams
Fucking advertising! God, I am a TECHNOLOGIST:
studiedforsixyearsyouwashedup Cursing! Another two years
for the job Nothing happened without me do you understand
NOTHING If I made a mistake everything came to a halt
I couldn't make one As soon as something didn't run
smoothly it was clear that something I had . . . I was the best

They never had a better I've got that In writing! – she screamed and tipped out the whole drawer Sure: I'll deliver the mail And then sometimes she's quite peaceful with you her head on my shoulder And she smells so good How she smells . . . God almighty already I don't know how she smelt any more . . . And I didn't mean it I can testify **I didn't** mean it Only stroked A bit And how she starts to laugh On my shoulder **She had laughed!** She often did that Suddenly she was cheerful again . . . so cheerful Out of the blue She was strong! Manisshestrong I've often thought! I thought that was weird It was w e i r d I thought! Often And I remember when she had finished: studying and the child and the parents always getting involved . . . And above all studying: she slams the book shut and laughs – I think you'll just have to screw me And suddenly she is laughing I really didn't mean it She did resist But then she always . . . she often did . . . She laughed: no no don't no stop it And ran Over the table if necessary and threw cushions and laughed: no no . . . Come you do want it And how it creaked She never wanted an upholstered bed They're for old-age pensioners she snorted with laughter – and clerks . . . On the edge she must . . . She never wanted But I didn't mean to! I was already inside And still she laughed and with her fists: stopityoubastard And all the upper part of her body with such strength **She was really strong!** She had her head so awkwardly . . . There was only one snapping noise Only one *feels the palm of his hand* Suddenly her chin went still But she was really strong? Wasn't she? If she hadn't laughed At least not laughed It was only fun . . . This snapping noise Always this snapping noise . . . It was easy And how I loved her !!! I knew immediately that she was dead I hadn't even shouted at her – incredibly – like in the films: **Jennif!** Jennif! *very quietly* Jennif! I knew at once We don't love them We don't love them at all All we love about them is our potential to destroy them I didn't love her I didn't mean to! Only my potential to break her It was so easy My God it was so easy One snapping noise I suddenly knew what a woman is I had broken her neck and then I knew what a woman is We break their necks and then we know . . . I suddenly loved her **Her** And it was too late.

VIII

LE GO – Child's Play

Brightly lit stage. A mother walking up and down nervously; over her clothing a light housecoat which she holds together over her chest. Downstage a rocking chair, white, with its back to the audience and constantly in motion although nobody can be discerned in it.

MOTHER. It need not have happened S h o u l d   n o t SHOULD NOT people will say Everyone will say it's my fault The neighbours my parents everyone HIS MOTHER! I'll never survive it *laughs as though about a mistake, pulls the coat together across her chest, then to the rocking chair:* Just keep still a moment will you Could I have had an inkling? An i n k l i n g! The child always begged: let me play with Kai come to my house sometime why can't he It got unbearable Will you keep still It's unbearable If the weather had at least been better It's not so bad outside And Walter wouldn't have had anything against And Walter didn't have anything against Kai and Jennifer . . . Played very nicely with each other Wellareyouplayingnicelywitheachother he said when he came back from the office And his boss: WellKaiareyouplayingnicely when he came back Usually somewhat earlier than Walter But not in the flat he said Walter We are agreed on that he said We are agreed on that in the office This private hobnobbing spoils the working atmosphere he said He had already wanted to move . . . If only that had worked out, it all wouldn't have happened But *pulling the coat together across her chest* first he would have had to have the new job But he h a d   n o t got it yet He **did not** have it yet *to the rocking chair* Can't you keep still? No? For a minute Kee-ep still . . . And the gun! I always said we don't need a thing like that Walter Walter, I said, us with a gun! You couldn't harm anyone anyway He must protect us *to the rocking chair* he meant US At the same time he would never have fired Never Not even if . . . And then he put it in a strong box Walter! Walter I said after that happened last summer: the gun is no use if you lock it up and I am alone and the child if someone makes trouble at the front door . . . In broad daylight! The windows were open upstairs, there was music in the sitting room! I nearly died of fright *screams* And if you are not even there! He said, Walter said, it all ended happily and it was a coincidence Coincidence? Don't you think it is always a coincidence when something like that happens The truth is one cannot arm oneself against coincidences Do you hear Walter And he said I should think of *to rocking chair* Look keep still dammit . . . think of the child and control myself After all nothing happened He didn't know how the lock worked and me and my hysteria Darling stop being hysterical darling he said I don't know when Walter put the thing in the wardrobe I really don't know I don't k n o w I saw it when I was tidying up Again and again When I was tidying up It didn't look at all dangerous I never touched it Tidied up things which were lying around it – yes . . . Walter's cigarettes handkerchiefs He always had this habit with used handkerchiefs. It was as though it was no longer there I had looked at it but I hadn't seen it any more Somehow S o m e h o w Not until I heard the muffled bang did I know that was a shot IMMEDIATELY I saw the gun immediately I hadn't thought anything of it, that the children were playing in the bedroom It was already tidy in there I always start with the bedroom My mother used to say that My mother always said never let anyone look on your unmade bed It reveals a slovenly nature They had taken everything with them The boards The building bricks What are the things called? I'm quite – For heaven's sake keep still just for once keep still . . . I'm confused I called to them once: DON'T BICKER! Jennifer's got even more of them I'll get them We've still got some We've got even more We have so many Then Christmas Grandparents always have to spoil children so . . . Ijustwanttohooverherequickly! . . . I knew at once that it was a shot I saw his mother immediately I n s t a n t a n e o u s l y My God, it shot through my head, whatever shall I tell his mother   I could still see her as she pushed the lad through the door How she had dressed up! Just to go the few steps We'vebeenlivingheresolong she said Kai is so bored and now it's raining so hard   Of course only if you don't mind   And I was only thinking of the child . . . It was also bored   Walter won't approve I thought   And the state of the child's room   CHAOS!   I always start with the bedroom Child, my mother would say, one look into the bedroom   betrays   the   character   of   a   woman Ridiculous simply ridiculous Still! Stillstillstill **Silence!** I read in a book a woman's hair betrays her character No Nono   God almighty how confused I am Her hair betrays the state of the bed   Of the bed −   Mother was always afraid I could turn out slovenly . . .   I needn't have sent them into the bedroom! Should not! SHOULD NOT!!   The way he looked at me the lad   One bullet would have been enough I didn't even have any more time to see my child   HOW WERE YOU LYING THEN?   One would have been enough I was dead immediately *the housecoat falls open as though by accident as the woman lets her arms fall in resignation, absentmindedly, blood stains on chest, stomach,   abdomen. Laughing:*   One would have been enough *furious*   It didn't even hurt!   I didn't do it! he screamed   Mummy!   he screamed   I didn't even have time to mourn   One must mourn one's child One should have at least mourned! Mourned   Do you hear?   It is unforgivable not to kill what one loves oneself. God doesn't forgive us if we don't do it ourselves . . . One **must** kill what one loves HE doesn't forgive us for what we don't kill − o u r s e l v e s *hauls out of the rocking chair an unclothed, child-size, very heavy doll-figure and drags it over the stage holding on to any one of its extremities*   It kills us.

IX

Deutschmeister or Fun and Transfiguration of Jennifer Klemm

Square with bus stops. A very young woman comes, gets out a book wrapped in newspaper, sits down. Nobody else. Suddenly left beside the stage, behind a door, a hissing argument. A struggle about opening the door, increasingly loud.

WOMAN'S VOICE. DistanceDistanceDistance . . . I can't **stand** hearing it any more! You can't give me a big enough salary to wipe me out. That's what you want isn't it? Isn't it? *louder* To kill me! everything that's ME – publicly of course . . . And all for so little money! . . .

MAN'S VOICE. Other people show their backsides for less money!

WOMAN'S VOICE. Oh yes? – Up till now, if I like someone, I have shown my backside for free, just so you know . . .

MAN'S VOICE. We'll play the diva once more, shall we? Anyway you haven't shown me anything for free yet . . . neither – if you please – your absence from the role nor your backside!

WOMAN'S VOICE. Exactly . . .

Someone slaps someone's face

MAN'S VOICE. Look for another stage for your amateurish appearances . . .

Another slapping of the face. The woman in the light housecoat from the previous scene comes through the door, turns round again:

WOMAN. Iamaamateuroflife, am I? . . . Do you know what you can't take? You cannot take it that **I** don't need a stage to secure my presence on this godforsaken earth, this hellish

province of the mind . . . I **act**, do you hear . . . I really act
and all the goddamm rest of it my biology takes care of . . .

*goes to leave through the emergency exit . . . followed by a
man*

MAN. You stay here! Do you hear! We can manage without
you . . . I w a n t you to act in it! . . . Your biology, OK . . .
Face facts! . . . Your excellently functioning biology will let
you know when you're a write-off! Do you understand! . . .
You can write that off! . . . *yells* We've got a contract, haven't
we !! . . . *throws the doll-figure after the woman, turns
around, goes fuming through the door beside the stage . . .
The whole scene unlit, while the very young woman at the
bus stop reads the wrapped book. From the back a group
of youths: two skinheads, a hanger-on, a proper young
German man, a girl in a bomber jacket and mini-skirt . . .*

CHORUS.   Lefties are marshmallows
                 Hang them on the gallows
                 Lefties are marshmallows
                 Hang them on the gallows . . .

PROPER YOUNG GERMAN. . . . Wait, I've got a new one:
Lefties are like maggots – lesbians and faggots . . .

general merriment

HANGER-ON *sits down very close to the very young woman.*
Eh wotcha reading?

FIRST SKIN. Let me see eh . . . *closes in on her from the other
side*

SECOND SKIN. Intellectual ladies . . . *burps in her face . . .*
Wouldn't you rather fuck, eh? Ladies who read don't fuck,
eh?

PROPER YOUNG GERMAN. Where have you been, man!
Germany needs intelligence. More than ever before. The final
victory needs an abundance of intelligence. Where, I ask you,
is it going to come from, if the potential German mother
doesn't educate herself? *to the very young woman:* Ignore
him. He's just drunk a bit too much . . . It's Gila's birthday.

FIRST SKIN. Yeah, – Right on, frustration. It's Gila's birthday and she can't today – *grabs the girl's mini-skirt* Right, Gila?

GILA. IdiotShitPissface – what's it got to do with you, eh?

SECOND SKIN. It's true, Gila-baby . . .

FIRST SKIN. . . . Gila-baby, don't be so 'crude' and look at this here. The woman is educating herself extremely usefully for our offspring . . . *puts his arm around the very young woman who is practically paralysed with fear*

GILA. Who knows what she's reading. Maybe she's reading about how to avoid your fucking offspring . . .

PROPER YOUNG GERMAN *strokes the practically paralysed very young woman's hair.* Leave her alone . . .

GILA. It's true . . . Let her read it aloud . . .

The very young woman clutches the book

PROPER YOUNG GERMAN. You must excuse them. They're not like this usually. Really good mates usually. But you could show us . . .

GILA. Man, are you soppy today . . . *snatches the book out of the very young woman's hands.*

HANGER-ON *takes the book out of the girl's hand and reads while the skinheads gringigglebawl.* . . . As nature in spring, naked, . . . lies down and as it were certain of victory . . . displays her delights . . . displays all her delights . . . while in winter she covers her shame and bareness . . . with snow and ice, so different is Luc – fuckinghell . . . Lucre-tius . . . Lucretius, the fresh, bold, poetic Lord of the World . . . Lord of the World, from Plutarch, who covers his small ego in the snow and ice of morality . . . *the skinheads finger at the coat of the nearly paralysed woman* . . . When we see an anxious, buttoned-up . . . *explosions of laughter* . . . anxious, buttoned-up, bowed individual, . . . we reach involuntarily for dress . . . for dress and buckle, to see if we too are still there . . .

SECOND SKIN *in the very young woman's face.* . . . Eh, we are still there too . . .

HANGER-ON. . . . and as it were fear losing ourselves. But at the sight of a merry joyjumper we forget ourselves and we feel exalted above our skin . . .

FIRST SKIN. Eh, feel here, my skin's about be exalted too . . .

GILA. You say that now – another three beers, you drip, and the hottest porno film won't get it up for you . . .

general merriment

HANGER-ON. . . . as universal powers and we breathe more boldy . . . Who feels more morally pure, freer, he who hails from the schoolroom of Plutarch, . . . **hails!** – totally hip eh . . . who hails from the school of Plutarch, . . . pondering on the injustice that the good lose the fruit of their lifetimes when they die, or he who sees eternity fulfilled, the bold, thundering song of Lucretius: . . . *further raising his voice* . . . Hoping for fame has powerfully shaken my mind. As with the staff of Thyrsus. And it awoke in my heart the sweetest desire for song. It drove me with a striving spirit. Impenetrable ways. To untrod domains of the muses. To wander through them. There is the joy of finding virgin sources out of which I create. There is the joy of plucking fresh-sprouting flowers and binding them. Into a glorious wreath for me. To wind around my head. Such as no one before has wound around his temples. The muses. For my song is of value from the first. Exalted things: I strive to. Further the mind from the bands of religion. To free further. My poetry enlightens the darkness. Of this terrain brightly. Because over the whole. The magic of the muses spreads . . . And further: . . . He who takes no more pleasure in building the whole world out of his own resources, in being a creator of the world *now increasingly captivated by the text* than wandering around in his own skin for ever, over him his mind has declared its anath-ema, he is overlaid with rest-rict-ion, but an inverted one, . . . he is driven out of the temple and from the eternal enjoyment of the mind and instructed to sing lullabies over his own private bliss and to dream about himself at night . . . Blessedness is not a reward for virtue, but is rather itself a virtue . . . bhabhabhaba, bhabhabhaba . . . : The prime basis of philosophical research is a bold free spirit! *snaps the books shut –*

FIRST SKIN. Completely incomprehensible . . .

SECOND SKIN. What's this highfalutin jabber?

PROPER YOUNG GERMAN. Why . . . Sounds very sensible.
You can think about it *to the skinheads* – if you can . . . *to
the very young woman* . . . really, we could use a woman like
you. We'll never get any further with Germany if the women
show no understanding for the Great – EXALTED. A strong
fatherland n e e d s pathos – the pathos of the mother *puts
his hand into the completely paralysed woman's coat,
looking at her as he does so* . . . Really –

GILA. Yack yack, you bums, – our bus!

*They run, jumping over the barriers between the bus stops.
The hanger-on chucks the book down at the very young
woman's feet. She: in shock. Staring ahead. Trembling. . . . A
man comes – apparently not German – ; he has fleetingly
observed the rest of the scene. He picks up the book, carefully
touches the seated woman – all very tenderly.*

NON-GERMAN. Ave say done anysing to you?   Har you
hokay?

WOMAN *trembling, absentminded.*

NON-GERMAN. Eet ees hokay . . . Do you hear . . . Say are
gone . . . *goes to give her the book, cleans off the over . . .*

WOMAN *miles away.* It was Marx . . . No . . . Yes . . . Yes, I'm
alright now . . . *looks at him* It w a s Marx . . .

NON-GERMAN *draws himself up; the look of a ruler; throws
the book beside her.* Har you a red under the bed? Yes?
bending down to her You Germans har a godless people. If
we 'ad henough to eat at home, we wouldn't set one foot on
your godless soil godless . . .

Leaves quickly, spitting.

*The very young woman remains: paralysed motionless. She
does not move – the embodiment of a bus stop.*

SHE C A N N O T MOVE.

X

The Hamlet-Machine

At the back the rubbish left over from previous scenes: the set of the room, the wind instruments; chairs, wall, doll etc.; the bus stop bench with the unmoving sitting woman. At the front several monitors; a big object like a box; a transparent box in which books are lying like lottery tickets waiting to be drawn.

A MAN GOES THROUGH THE RUINS OF THE PLAY –

picks up something, throws it aside carelessly; picks up something else – as though he was looking for something specific of which he knows nothing. Downstage in a storm of flashlights a woman: clerk.

CLERK *stares at the monitor in front of her.* My name is . . .

LOUDSPEAKER. Once more please. Left.

CLERK *turns around.* My name is –

LOUDSPEAKER. The left camera please. . . . Once more.

CLERK *turns back, looking tensely into the left monitor.* My name . . .

LOUDSPEAKER. Jesus, it won't eat her . . . once more, – Go . . .

CLERK. –

LOUDSPEAKER. Go now – Camera!

CLERK. My name is Melanie Howman   I introduce   I'm supposed to I mean well we have   Well I work in a library And we had a big problem with the questions   I mean our readers had the problem with the questions   We had an author . . . we had engaged an unemployed writer   But it was very difficult with him   He made continual demands for

conditions and books Books and conditions . . . So that he
could answer the readers' questions He needed a colossal
number of books And the simpler the questions were the
more books he needed At first he had sat in the foyer Well
in our entrance-hall He sat there and nobody saw him
Because he was completely walled in by books And how he
s c r e a m e d! as soon as anybody took one **so much as one**
away! For example one reader Because he mistook his book
environment for the media units which belong in our stock . . .
When someone, whose question had previously qualified, put
this same through a sort of letter-box, out came – if all went
well – an answer from a sort of throw-out-tray But mostly
new questions came out From the castle of books On the
whole the people were pleased When the questions were
taken off them Which they hadn't even asked! They ran out
of them you see The questions I mean the people ran out of
questions They had to read so much and then were still not
sufficiently qualified for the questions he demanded . . . HE
HAD BECOME A MOLOCH Immoderate! in his demands
We were supposed to supply him with LIFE He said he
couldn't work otherwise . . . To be honest: we'd had him up
to here . . . At first we only delivered his food Later women
Then only the news about everything That was even more
strenuous **This continual news-bringing** About the food
About the women About the news We **hated!** his need for
information He put us under per – ma – nent stress All of
us Still we couldn't do anything about it The people were
addicted to their problem with the questions And they were
addicted to his problem with their unasked questions It
seemed to remind them of something which must be
nearanddear to them . . . Anyway **we** had the leg work to do
So that the people had enough problems to chew over I mean
sufficient problems They had food and relationships and
media units . . . But no problems! And when one thinks that
we did all this free of charge! . . . It doesn't bear thinking
about – *pause* We then sat down together There were experts
there too Criticspeopleinpoliticsineconomics – NOTHING
IS FOR FREE – We needed sponsors . . . The breakthrough
came through a psychologist When we were close to having
to capitulate to the problem with this Moloch He gave us the

vital clue: We should ask the monster ourselves! . . . The Moloch occupying our entrance-hall He was addicted to job justification There was no question which stimulated him more than the question of abolishing himself . . .

He directed our attention to scientific institutions which have to do with physics In the broadest sense MathematicsBio-chemistryCybernetics and stuff like that Interdisciplinary! We didn't grasp it quite . . . The result was this problem analysing machine It is . . . It splits every simple component into a constellation of at least two dimensions **At least!** You put in an answer and the machine finds at least one question One might almost say compulsive! . . . You chuck – er throw a book in *demonstrates* here and it filters you out at least two user-friendly problems   Guaranteed   *short pause*   Our working party received . . . *to upstage* Should I say that is well? . . .

LOUDSPEAKER *somewhat muffled.* God in heaven, this stupid old bag . . . What does she think she's here for!

CLERK. Well our working party received a major award for this in the biggest German research competition   And the supporting grant from the Association of Publishing-related Employers *now expertly professional* – The machine is cost-effective, space-saving and works independently of how qualified the questions are which are posed. According to currently available calculations it scarcely requires any information. The trial run which has yet to be . . . Well I Well they've – They have entrusted me with the honourable task as the youngest and *with some pride* only female member of the working party of undertaking the trial run here in public – I am proud of the fact herewith trial run – Well I shall well, herewith, by introducing an ar *rummages in the clear container which stands at the ready* bi tr ar y medium *throws in a novel or similar* and my name *aloud as she types in* Name – Me la nie How man . . . start up the trial run – *the machine begins to work, sheets of paper fly out of an opening, the clerk collects them up* . . . ceremoniously. *she indicates a curtsey and does not know what to do with the paper* – I thank you for you . . . *the machine goes on producing paper; it is virtually impossible to gather up any more and falls out of the clerk's arms which are making every effort to restore order –*

LOUDSPEAKER. OK. Cut and out. Take five . . . And for God's sake don't take her profile. Let them edit the text in underneath, I wash my hands of . . .

Goes off the air.

The flashlights vanish. Stage hands clear away the monitors. The machine works. Synthesis of the sound of printer and keyboard. The clerk tries to switch off the machine. She presses a few buttons. The machine works. She presses every button. The machine works. She runs in despair around the box. The machine works. She tears through cables. The machine works. Clears aside mountains of paper. . . .

Meanwhile MAN *in the ruins of the play has found something. He stands fascinated* IN FRONT OF *the sitting* WOMAN, *as though he had an idea; he stands her up painstakingly, carries the bus stop bench downstage, straightens it carefully.*

Fetches the very young woman who is now standing; carries her as though she were precious; sits her on the floor with her back against the bench.

He goes upstage again to fetch the tuba; parts the legs of the seated woman; positions the tuba; then upstage again. After some searching, he puts the telephone into the opening of the instrument and winds the very long cable round the seated woman; regards his work . . . Again vaguely searching in the ruins, but visibly content . . .

THE CLERK *squats* IN FRONT OF THE MACHINE, *her hands over her ears; something occurs to her as though she is remembering a great catastrophe . . .*

She gabbles. She quotes. She declaims. Screams. Sings. Scolds. WeirdWhine Whimpers. It is a hatred. A mourning. A whispering a grinning. A LAUGHTER. Threatening. EXTRAVAGANT GESTURES.

Overflowing: A despair which believes in itself.

The machine works.

CLERK.
On the day when we had finished
Thinking through the invention . . .
And everything was gone
That morning: The whole high castle
Stacks of knowledge
Piled up high we had
Continually thrown
In provisional results
The commentaries increasingly
Pitiful got so
That we thought: SOMEONE
LIKE THAT ONE could hold us
In sway in power in
FASCINATION
Until this morning when the Absurd
Nothing: Laughed
People puffed out lips
For another purpose: For screaming
A non-sensical yelling unheard
Of they skinned each others'
Foreheads with iron and hammers
They beat the sign
From out of their heads
Coiting in broad daylight
They devoured each other
And all that halfway
Resembled them: Thus swept
The bloody prize of baseless order
Through the whole first edition
Of the Memoryhall AND
Nobody heard what
I could hear: sound of
This voice sound of
This dread whispering sound
From allaround ANDANDAND

Whispering from all around: AND AND AND

CLERK. But there must be one word left over FOR US!

She jumps up, takes her shoe off, hammers on the machine with the heel. As though beside herself.

The machine works.

The man out of the ruins; watches the clerk.

CLERK.
Language is a punishment
With no warranty
THE WORD maintains itself
In pain without a name
The shame about our nakedness
About which we speak
                              And speak
                                        And speak
These mouths from all around
Opening around us: Dumbly
These ears are twisting to perceive
ONE WORD: draught
In labyrinths of deep
Mourning: Ice cold breath
Which splits the eyelids
The lightning
It takes to search the lips for the
Answer to unlock the riddle
To find out the mystery:
These mouths all around
With their wandering senseless opening
And from everywhere dread dread
Full of whispering –

This whispering from all around.

These mouths with their senseless opening.

CLERK. into we're SPEAKING S P E A K I N G S P E A K
I N G . . . *hammers on the machine with her heel*

The machine works.

MAN. The truth value of our language is reduced to AND.
Within this *touches her face with interest turning it carefully*
we have to conduct ourselves. – Have you got a role too?

CLERK. What are you doing there?

MAN. I am collecting. *While he further investigates her useful-ness:* What history throws off I pick up. And drop . . . According to laws of aesthetics. I have the control *presses an apple into her hand* over evidence. The events are not the most important thing; it is the evidence about events. I play a role . . . *pointing to the shoe* . . . What are you doing there?

CLERK. And all the time you know what you are doing there?

MAN. Were I not to do this, I should at no time know that I am doing anything that all . . . *lifts her hand holding the apple* . . . I like you. You are such an innocent . . . *turns her skull again* . . . – child . . .

CLERK. I don't know if I'm playing a role. It would mean following a certain logic. I try to proceed illogically. This demands enormous concentration It's almost more than I can cope with I don't like you *throws the apple away* . . .

MAN. –

CLERK. Do you think they burn if you put them in your mouth? There must be ONE word for **US** . . . *he turns away* . . . If you put the words in your mouth and swallow? *calls* Do you think so? If you are playing a role, then you must know?! . . . *lies down in the mountains of paper in front of the machine; despairingly holding her ears out of which wax is dripping; between her fingers the wax* . . .

The man turns again to the sitting woman, regarding his work complacently.

MAN. The decayed shores alone bear witness to the beauty of the absurd . . . *getting out the lipstick he has found and putting it thickly on to the sitting woman's mouth* . . . The cancer of society reeks on the pictures formed of mould which multiply from one exhibition to the next . . . *uncovers one of her breasts, crushes the rest of the lipstick in his hand and puts the tough mass on the naked part* . . .

MAN *stroking her hair, tender, full of awe.* How beautiful you are. If only you could s e e yourself. It is extra-ordinarily beautiful . . . *when he slowly detaches himself from working on her appearance, ready to go:* When you have devoured the ruins of Europe you will bring forth wonderful cripples, regenerate COMPLETELY degenerate organisms, covered with a fabulous greygreen weave – Humans excrete what they eat you know –

It is inevitable that you will discharge the perfect likeness of the events you have devoured. And it will be **beautiful** like everything that is perfect And we shall **both** have created it *whispers* **We are God!** – *leaves, going past the machine, which works; climbing over the clerk.*

MAN *to the clerk, from above.* If you want to save the fire, you have to set the library alight beforehand . . . Do what you want with the words. Swallow them for all I care . . . You may die that way. That would be b e a u t i f u l – aesthetic to a degree – I like you but I can't do anything with you . . . *kicks the unremittingly working machine, leaves the play . . .*

The clerk sits up slowly.

This whispering from all around.
These mouths senselessly opening.
This despair which believes in itself.

This predicament of speech which has always already begun.

CLERK. If we don't save the fire we don't feel any pain if we have no memories we cannot see what we are MONSTROUS! You have invented all games till the world lies silent For he who created it has gone to rest But *screams* my memory IS Inhuman *holding her ears, declaiming; affirmative* Even if I am a poor whore my heart inflames with the song Song Song *Song **Rosenkranz and Guildenstern – like you it's not my hologram** . . . suddenly takes her hands away from her ears* Saying everything and not wanting to hear ANYTHING is a kind of COVETOUSNESS: **IWASHAMLET** and when in doubt loved myself **Established** in sinews of longing for dwelling in my veins . . . *as in Brecht/Weill* **LORD JESUS CHRIST BE OUR GUEST and b l e s s what you have be stow ed on us** . . . From the day he was born his name was glorious Two thirds of him are God   A third A third only human . . . When you had no more ideas about your life   Then you

spoke truly **But only then!** . . . Good I hoped   There came
unhappiness   I awaited light   The darkness drew near
thedarknessdrewneardrewneardear – DREAM: A dream is
everything To be And the dreams themselves are dream . . .
D r e a m . . . **and what they don't keep today** won't even
be promised tomorrow *now like recapitulating a school
lesson* Besmirched by their speech . . . Their language Used
as a cover for earthly goods   THUS *declaims* no sensible
person will dare to clothe what he thinks in this weak
language And certainly not in immovable form: This life-
warm feeling motion shrinks to a clod . . . **t o m e** . . . YOU
MONSTERS! *screaming* **My peace** . . . *sings* **andnever-
more shallfindit nevermoreshall findit** *raving against the
machine* You have invented ALL allallall A L L games Alas
No one could play that well and yet   In your cumbersome
bodies lies your delicacy . . . **Holy** All things are holy Father
paint me the earth   Upon my body go your songs Inhuman is
my memory: The hour sparkles and has a shape . . . **Already**
the worldisvisible through your body Transparently clear in
a flash through your clarity **Already** my inhuman memory
is **already** my liver is senseless . . . when will my heart –
myheartisheavy – my heart be senseless *laughs, l a u g h s*
Heartmy heart You will fall away from me later Like you
were only tacked on Of parchmentpaper We hunt the brain
Out of our skulls And the knife in our bodies . . . What I think
no longer blossoms out of my skin . . . *gradually calmer* My
cerebrum is a landscape in the fog A swamp which floods
Warm veil over cold smooth stones which look to it to forget
U n b e l i e v i n g l y I stare at my menstrual blood A person
is not fleshbonesjuices but sentences leprosy of his restless
mind **A PER SON IS SEN TEN CES** . . . WORDS bleed
from my mouth . . . You will be able to read my shroud like a
newspaper . . .

. . .

. . .

The fighter bombers of modernity circle over my Indian
knowledge Vultures in joyless waiting

. . .

It is raining birds

. . .

Esundesiertocircularelmundo

el cielo

está cerrado

y el infierno

. . . vacio

. . .

The machine works.

The clerk goes to the sitting woman, tries to wipe the lipstick off her; gently to her as though calming herself:

CLERK. A countenance that could look into the sun . . . has never been known from time immemorial . . . *frees the sitting woman from the cable, sits down next to her, leans her head on her shoulder . . .*

CLERK. Are you playing a role? – You are surely playing a role. He has lent you meaning . . . *calm, alarming calm* Hold a snake hold still so that my sister can paint your beautiful colours . . .

CLERK. Why don't you say anything . . .

WOMAN. I know the world so scarcely, I understand it.

The machine works.

The stage full of papers. End.

The machine works behind the curtain. The continuous and unbearable noise, a mixture of printer and keyboard. Even when the curtain opens again the machine is working in the darkness of the stage.

The audience hurries out of the auditorium. The machine works.

Louder. Louder and louder . . .

Louder.

Even when the auditorium has completely emptied itself the machine works.

THE MACHINE WORKS.

ITS MEMORY IS HUMAN.

Notes on Theory and Play Practice

a)   As an introduction, the following pieces of music are recommended to be played in parallel to each other:
 1.   A recording of 'Welcome to the United States' by Mr Frank Zappa with the ENSEMBLE MODERN.
 2.   From: Giuseppe Verdi, Messa de Requiem, VII – LIBERA ME the passage about:
 Tremens factus sum ego / et timeo /
 dum discussi venerit, atque /
 ventura ira / Dies irae, dies illa, /
 Calamitatis et miseriae /
 (repeat continuously to the end of 1.)

b)   I and II should be played in one scene for the sake of speed.

c)   III = Shares in the state of the art.

d)   It is advisable to do the audience the courtesy of putting in a COMMERCIAL BREAK between VII and VIII which gives it the opportunity briefly to indulge its habits: it should be able to urinate without anxiety, sip champagne or switch off; which means giving it the chance to leave the performance in the theatre prematurely but discreetly.

e)   A suggestion for the staging: the interval ritual is introduced by beach balls which are thrown gracefully into the audience by the available theatre staff. A slide projection appears on the closed set: the advertisement of a big postcard publisher from south Germany. We read: 'Many animals have a highly developed family life . . . ! Observe them and you will be moved.' We see: the stage is the picture of a female gorilla with young . . . (Further suggestions for staging on request: please enclose a stamped, addressed envelope.)

f)   GRAMMAR CHOREOGRAPHS THE ACT OF SPEECH

g) SENTENCE: LANGUAGE IS THE HOLOGRAM OF OUR FEELING AND THINKING. EVEN WHERE IT IS REDUCED TO THE EXTREME: ALL INFORMATION ABOUT ITS ENTIRETY WILL BE CONTAINED DOWN TO ITS LAST WORD. EVEN IN THAT SILENCE IN WHICH LANGUAGE BINDS ITSELF, THE CONTEXT IS C O M P L E T E L Y VISIBLE. LANGUAGE HAS TO BE CONCEPT <u>AND</u> THING AT THE SAME TIME, TO MAKE IT IMPOSSIBLE FOR US NOT TO FEEL A ND THINK. THUS CREATION IS DENOTED BY **THE WORD** AS THE ETERNAL BEGINNING. THERE IS NO NEW CREATION: ONLY A SELF-CONTAINING MEMORY OF <u>THE</u> CREATION, WHICH WE GAIN OUT OF THE LOSS OF CONTEXT.

h) The list of notes about the sources of quotations adopted, used and consciously recalled in word/behaviour/sound/image can be requested separately. (stamped, addressed anvelope !)

i) A key to the characters and their varying entrances can be requested separately. (!)

WHERE THE FRAMEWORK OF PLAY IS NO LONGER VISIBLE BEGINS THE DANGER.